The
Single
Solution

The Single Solution

by

Donna M. Cowan

New Leaf Press

ISBN: 0-89221-319-1
Library of Congress Catalog: 95-73131

All personal names given in the illustrations in this book are changed.

Dedication

This book is dedicated to Bill Stone. You are my soul mate, and your support and love have sustained me during times of testing. I look forward to the destiny you have in my life. I love you Bill.

Thanks

So many people to thank, so little space.

I'm positive he will be shocked by this, but I particularly thank my first husband, Roger. Although he walked out on our marriage, he was responsible for my salvation. He would not be married to a non-Christian, so I agreed to become one, whatever that meant. Thanks, too, to the pastor at the small church who understood my questions, and after a few leading questions asked me, "If Jesus is real, do you want Him in your life?" Following a sincere prayer, though filled with doubts, Jesus accepted my invitation.

Thanks to Harry Odum, author of *The Vital Singles Ministry,*[1] a dear friend, who told me how to market my manuscript and whose advice assisted me more than he will ever know.

Thanks to all the fantastic Christian television evangelists who were there to lift my spirits at all hours of the day and night, especially Pat Robertson and his cohorts at the "700 Club," and Paul and Jan Crouch with all their co-hosts throughout the years.

To Josh McDowell, Hal Lindsey, Joyce Meyer, Malcolm Smith, Ken Copeland, Marilyn Hickey, Jesse DuPlantis, Rick Renner, Jerry Savelle, Richard and Oral Roberts, Charles Stanley, James Dobson, Chuck Colson, and so many other Christian teachers and authors, thanks for the time you have spent sharing your faith to build mine.

Thanks to one of my pastors, Billy Joe Daughtery, who taught me the power of the Word, and who is the founder of Victory Bible Institute where I learned so much about God.

Thanks to my other pastor, Bob Piersen, who taught me

compassion and acceptance. There is no pastor anywhere who has more love, care, and concern for the single person than does Dr. Bob. He is to me the epitome of a pastor who walks as Jesus would walk.

A special thanks to Sharon Daughtery for her excellent suggestions on the format of this book, all of which were instituted. Her suggestions made for a more organized and powerful manual that can be a useful tool for years.

Thanks to all my friends who contributed to this book through their comments and anecdotes: Betty, Renee, Howard, Julie, Bob, Cheryl, Charlene, James, Maureen, Marylou, and so many, many more it would be impossible to name them all.

Thanks to all my family for their support during my years of "training and testing," especially Harold and Wanda Meyer, Dale and Sue VanZant, Marylouise and Howard Cowan, Jack Meyer, Joe and Betty Meyer, and my beloved grandparents, Sudie and Will Meyer. I love you all.

Thanks to my daughter, Stacey Renee Cowan, who has been my friend and my heart. I love you, darling. I am so very thankful you have the privilege of knowing Jesus so much sooner than I did so I can rest in that knowledge as you embark on your life as an adult.

And a special thanks to "Charles," who was the instrument God used to teach me such a valuable lesson.

And, of course, thanks so much, Jesus, for accepting my sincere, though doubting, invitation to come into my life. Without You, Jesus, I am nothing, but with You I can do all things. I am so blessed, and I owe it all to You.

TABLE OF CONTENTS

Foreword

Donna Cowan has presented, in a clear, biblical, and spiritual manner, one of the major issues facing single women today. With the continued high rate of divorce, single women are forced to confront issues of their sexuality and sexual relationships unprecedented for women in history. Donna has clearly outlined the dilemma.

With frank accounts depicting her own struggle and the struggles of many others, Donna has illustrated the afflictions of millions of women. The change of standards brought on by the so-called new morality has supposedly freed men and women, but in reality it has created a fearful situation in terms of sexually transmitted diseases, unwanted pregnancies and abortions, as well as a significant moral dilemma — and these problems don't begin to touch upon the harm to the person's spirit.

Men and women today are dealing with natural drives and needs that God has placed in each of us as part of His creation, and they must deal with a new sense of responsibility and creativity. Donna's presentation of the situation and consequences of extra-marital sex give us an understanding of what is facing today's single person. Her careful analysis of the devastation of sex outside of marriage and her affirmation of celibacy for singles provides a needed alternative to the promiscuity presented by contemporary American media and culture.

While the presentation not only shows a strong understanding of the dilemma, Donna also presents a biblical understanding of marriage.

As pastor of a large United Methodist Church where 40 percent of our membership are single persons, I am very much aware that this issue of sexual relationships is not simply a matter of whether to have sex outside of marriage, but it is a whole issue of personal identity, morality, and the standards on which we base our decisions. The large part of the American population who are single face a whole series of choices that affect their character, their vocation, and their values. In the past decisions were made based upon tradition or group pressure, customs and practices of family life. Today the situation is radically different. Each individual must make their own choices, and the pressure to live in a lifestyle that is opposed to their own ideals is sometimes overwhelming. These questions are raised in this book and must be dealt with by the contemporary single person and society as a whole.

Donna's affirmation of the strength we can gain from the power of God in our lives is one which can provide encouragement, understanding, and a plan for single women and men today. And the biblically based steps for guidance outlined in this book can be transferred to any area of life. Our faith in God and the insight into human responsibility presented by Jesus Christ in His teachings provide the answers. The sense of direction given by Jesus provide the basis for our making moral, responsible, caring, sensible decisions.

In the years to come, singles, desiring to live full, productive lives, will find there is a greater need to establish a value system. Only a faithful relationship with God can provide a refuge and a cornerstone for a fulfilling existence, and such a relationship empowers each individual who finds it to experience a life of joy, happiness, and satisfaction.

This book helps the reader with one of the most difficult decisions a single person must face and offers a creative, biblically sound conclusion and direction. Donna reminds us that we can do all things through Him who strengthens us! I believe that in reading this book and carefully asking what Jesus would do in the situations faced by singles, there is provided an insight and understanding of the situation and a solution. As you read through the book, the challenge is clearly presented — follow God's will and find the peace, satisfaction, and power that comes from a positive Christian life.

Dr. Robert Pierson, Senior pastor
Christ United Methodist Church, Tulsa, Oklahoma

Prologue

Sex! It's fun. And it is a blessing from God.

But I am single. And I am a Christian. People tell me sex outside of marriage is wrong — but I want a man in my life. I want romance and the intimacy of sex.

But I am single.

What do I do?

Do I learn to live without a man?

Do I *want* to?

Why do I want a man when I am content single?

Do I live without sex if I choose to remain single?

Do I *want* to?

If I refuse sex will any man stay with me long enough to develop a relationship leading to marriage?

Or do I decide living a Christian lifestyle is just too hard and give it all up? What happens, then, to my other beliefs about my faith? After all, if one part of my faith is too hard to live in the real world, then is any of it relative?

Decisions! Always decisions. Which to make?

Where do I go for answers?

* * *

I am not alone. Millions of single Christian women struggle with this dilemma. What is God's will for a single Christian woman? Why does she want a man in her life? What does she do about sex?

A lady in my Sunday school class said, "After my divorce I found myself making sexual decisions I never thought I would ever have to make. When I was married I didn't have a clue what it was going to be like as a single. What does a single

Christian woman do about sex?"

This book was written because I could find nothing to help me make sexual decisions as an "experienced woman." As "experienced women" we have knowledge unknown to the virgin. We *know* what we are missing.

This book was written because other women would come to me for answers. I had no solutions. There was no place to refer them, no material I could find specifically for single women, specifically written by a woman who understood these women's issues because she'd "been there." We're not talking strictly theory, we're talking application.

This book is written in three sections: the first dealing with the dilemma facing single women, the second deals with revelations, and the third with solutions.

Single women today are learning together. As a whole, women of the fifties did not deal with this problem. When my parents divorced in the early sixties, they were the only divorced couple we knew.

Experienced single women today are stumbling through a learning curve without family role models, without mentors, without reference material, without established customs . . . but *not* without guilt.

Perhaps my story will help you as a single woman — a divorced woman, a widowed woman, or a woman who has been involved in an intimate relationship. Perhaps the case studies and reference material will help you make sexual decisions you can live with and you can accomplish. You are not alone.

Section One: The Dilemma

Chapter 1

The Word of My Testimony

No excuses. I knew it was wrong. My conscience said so.

At 40-something, you would think I had learned a thing or two. Single for nearly four years, I ached for a man's arms around me again, a man to care for and to care for me. I longed to experience once again the passion of sex with a man I love, to fall asleep in his embrace.

After four years, I had about given up on finding someone. Were my expectations too high? I wanted someone Christian and I wanted someone to whom I was physically attracted. Were the two mutually exclusive? Attractive, confident heathens did abound. Christian men were around, but none who could have come close to being the spiritual head of my household. Or if they did come close, they were not also interested in me.

Was I destined to be alone?

Then Charles entered my life. Charles, with all the behaviors and character traits of a southern gentlemen, appeared one morning at Sunday school. Surely God answered my prayers.

Our first date we went to the movie *Always*. Charles held

my hand, squeezing softly during passionate screen kisses. Occasionally he would lift my hand to his lips and there place a gentle kiss. To this day, five years later, I cannot hear the movie's theme song, "Smoke Gets In Yours Eyes," without my heart aching — aching to relive those memories, aching for the impossible dreams.

Charles treated me with love. Love like I have never felt before or since.

Unaccustomed to the kindnesses of a true gentleman, Charles took pleasure in teaching me. He would not let me open my own doors, car or otherwise. He helped me in and out of the car or my chair or a building. He held my coat. He held my hand. He called to make sure I made it home okay and to wish me a good night. He called to let me know he arrived home without incident and to tell me he loved me. If we were in a restaurant, he would buy me a single rose. He would not let me pay for anything anytime. He made the decisions, after consulting with me, about what to do and where to go.

He was strong, he was masculine, he was confident, he was decisive. He was everything I had ever wanted in a man. He was a man, not a wimp. He was a gentleman.

Charles and I talked for hours and hours about everything and anything. We talked about our marriages and how they had failed. We talked about our careers and our friends. We were open and honest about everything. He told me things I am sure he had never told anyone. We talked about God, our families, our world.

I remember the first time Charles told me he loved me. We were not yet intimate. Sitting at his kitchen table New Year's Eve after an evening of party hopping, Charles took my hand, looked into my eyes, and said, "I love you."

"You don't know me that well," I stated, dumbfounded. "How can you say that?"

"Donna," he said in a deep, masculine voice that sent my heart into overdrive, "I love you."

"Please, don't say that unless you mean it," I asked of him.

"I love you," he said in reply.

The strange thing? I loved him, too. So soon? How could

that be? Fate? Was God involved? I believed so.

Shortly, after I fell in love, I fell into his bed.

Still, no excuses.

After we succumbed to the subtle seduction of "making love," we dated for six of the sweetest weeks of my life.

Together we attended church and Sunday school. He stood by me when I taught classes. He encouraged me in my Bible study. Together we attended class socials. Charles told me one of the problems with his ex-wife was she would not attend church. If he attended church during his 20-plus-year marriage, he attended alone. He said he resented that.

We discussed marriage. Charles told me what he wanted in a marriage, and the word pictures he painted of my fantasy future were filled with visions from my childhood daydreams. My future seemed secure, just as I imagined long ago playing house on warm summer days. I still wanted to believe in the white picket fence, the two or three children, and the household where "Father Knows Best."

Before Charles, I presumed a traditional marriage was extinct. With Charles, for a moment in time, I believed things could be different. Hearing his words and visualizing the family portraits generated by those words, I did no longer doubt.

No question. God, indeed, brought Charles into my life. He was God's gift to me. I felt justified.

Charles was the consummate gentleman. He was my hero. He was my love.

Constantly he would utter, "This is too good to be true." And it was good. Outstanding. My dreams fulfilled in reality. I could find nothing wrong with him or with our relationship. All was perfect.

Our common interests were extraordinary. We both enjoyed going to the lake. He had a wonderfully cozy cabin where we spent New Year's Day, our first time together. On the tape deck we played Carol King's *Tapestry* album over and over as we cuddled. The icy-cold winter weather could not diminish the warmth of our love.

We learned that we liked to play bridge, we liked to walk, we liked to dance, we liked to read. He liked my friends and I liked his. We liked to be with our children. His daughters and my daughter quickly became fast friends.

We worked well together. He helped me move. I helped him around his house. We shopped for furniture together. We planned parties together. We looked at automobiles together. He even liked my cooking.

* * *

Unfortunately, Charles was right. The relationship did not last — so it was too good to be true.

Charles left. I was his transitional woman. Everything he told me was a mirage, seeming so real, yet vanishing upon a closer inspection.

Charles said he never wanted to hurt again like he hurt when his wife left him. He said he cared for me too much. He did not tell the truth. I knew that as sure as I knew my name. He told me what he wanted me to hear to soften the blow. I'll give him credit . . . he was concerned about me. The problem? The way he left things I always had hope when there was no hope.

When Charles left, I did not feel loved, even though he told me he loved me. I felt used. Not always a Christian, I had been intimate before in a relationship without the benefit of marriage. And, yes, I felt guilty then. But this time the fact of my new Christian birth multiplied manyfold the feelings I had of being used and abused.

I suffered for nearly two years after Charles. I dreamed of him every night, and I did not sleep through the night for months. I could not simply go for a drive without driving by his office or his house hoping to catch a glimpse of him. Just to hear him, I called his office in the middle of the night to listen to his answering machine. The deep resonance of his voice would send a charge, like electricity, tingling up and down my spine. Hearing the sound would soothe my shattered nerves, providing a momentary feeling of closeness.

The weight of oppression was an anvil around my neck. I could not believe a loving God would put this man in my life only to take him away. I could not believe that a loving God would allow my love for this man to demolish my heart.

For nearly two years I prayed without ceasing for Charles

to return. I claimed his return. And if God did not bring Charles back, could He please wipe any thoughts out of my mind?

If God answered prayers based on determination and will power, it would happen. I was determined.

God never did wipe Charles out of my mind. But return he did. God answered my prayers.

When Charles came back our relationship immediately reverted to what it had been before. This time, however, I was different. God dealt with me during Charles's absence, conforming me to the image of His Son. "And we know that in all things God works for the good of those who love him, who have been called according to his purpose. For those God foreknew he also predestined to be conformed to the likeness of his Son, that he might be the firstborn among many brothers" (Rom. 8:28-29).

An inner voice kept telling me, "Don't do it, Donna. This isn't right." But for months my flesh argued and won. The pleasures of sin for a season, the instant gratification, ignored the pain I had when he left before. Like the pain of having a baby is worth it, you rationalize this, too.

And I knew he would leave again. I just knew. I knew I would suffer again. I just knew.

We dated again for six months. Our practice was to see each other once or twice a week. Even though I still loved Charles beyond distraction, eventually this time I was able to resist the tormenting temptation to continue the sexual sin.

I went by his house one night as he requested. We sat in his living room sharing the activities of the week. As the evening came to a close, he began to kiss me and caress me as had become our custom. This time I said "No." This time I meant it. Charles understood. Charles accepted the situation. As always, the gentleman.

When I said "No," I almost felt and heard God pat me on the back and say, "Well done, child, well done."

The inner voice strengthened my resolve. My decision to do what was right was rewarded with God's determination to help me. I knew I could not resist alone. I knew that I would succumb if left to my own devices. But I had surrendered this area to Him.

Charles and I remained friends after my decision, continuing to have dinner occasionally, but not long afterwards Charles transferred out of state. Was his move God's way of taking away the temptation? I like to believe it was.

This time Charles leaving affected me differently. I felt pure and forgiven — not used. I felt cleansed — not abused.

After choosing to turn from temptation, God honored my decision by helping me follow through. As I prayed, "Lead me not into temptation, but deliver me from evil," God has performed His Word.

The result?

Joy!

* * *

What lessons did I learn from this experience?

The answers are significant and not easily discerned. The search for answers took many turns, but always led back to the Bible.

God wanted me to understand His love, not just His correction; and my research confirms Christian women everywhere need this revelation.

Chapter 2

Thelma

What about other women? Did God lead them in the same way? Would other women gain from reading the information in this book?

Days after reading the first draft of this book, Thelma faced her first trial. Jay, the love of her life, a professing Christian, and the man Thelma prayed over for seven years, appeared on her doorstep after a year's absence.

Have you ever had one of the situations in your life when you prayed over something so much and so often you were absolutely positive it was going to come about . . . but it did not? After a seven-year relationship and a year's separation, this was Thelma's state of mind. She was sure God had not heard her prayers.

Finally, Jay did return. Thelma was convinced this was God's doing and His will for her life. Claiming he wanted to marry her, Thelma knew God had finally worked on Jay and had answered her prayers.

Conforming to a well-established pattern where Jay was concerned, Thelma quickly yielded to her physical desires. And based on what Jay said that night, he wanted to make a commitment. She felt justified. Even after reading the material in this book, she felt justified.

Based on what Jay said that night, Thelma expected him to behave as her betrothed.

It did not happen.

Jay did not bother to call Thelma for over a week. He wanted to make a commitment all right, but it was not to Thelma. He married another woman within a month.

Thelma felt humiliation and shame. Thelma felt hurt to the point of mortal wounding — she did not want to live. She might have felt these emotions even had she not indulged, but the physical joining and sexual passion magnified the suffering many times.

If only she had walked away with her dignity. If only she retained her self-respect.

After this episode, Thelma asked God for help. Never strong willed concerning sex, Thelma enjoys sex a lot. Swayed with pretty words and gentlemanly conduct, it is obvious to her friends that Thelma craves confirmation of her femininity.

She is not alone. Many divorced women feel less than feminine because of the things faced as a single. The pressure on women to react in business situations in an aggressive and "manly" manner only aggravates the situation.

Women crave the affection only a man can give; only a man has the ability to make a woman feel cherished. Bottom line — a woman feels most like a woman when a man is around.

There was a time Thelma truly believed she would not and could not be happy unless she had a man in her life. That was before what she now calls the "Jay Episode." Thelma never hurt the way she hurt when Jay left.

Now, before allowing the involvement of her body or her heart, Thelma wants to be positive the relationship is permanent. She wants marriage first. Thelma wants joy, not pain. She wants happiness, not sorrow.

Concerning sex, marriage increases the odds of joy and happiness. *Sex outside of marriage increases the odds of pain and sorrow.*

Besides, which has God's blessing?

Thelma changed. She prays now: "Lead me not into temptation." She allows Jesus to love her as no man ever could. She trusts God, and He has been true to His Word. He has consistently maneuvered her away from hazardous situations, away from sexual temptation.

When gentlemen call, men to whom she finds herself physically attracted, but all wrong for her spiritually, Thelma, without exception, is away from the house. When others tempt her, she has the gumption to say, "No, thanks, I can't."

Thelma began dating Rex. The relationship looked possibly permanent. Rex insinuated many times he wanted to be with Thelma intimately. Thelma was tempted. Yet, because the Lord, at Thelma's invitation, had charge over this area of her life, He took charge.

Thelma and Rex made plans, but invariably the plans were botched.

Thelma and I were sitting around her dinner table one night when she related this story. The joy was obvious on her face. I had never seen her like this before.

Thelma tells that one night, while out dancing with friends, she overheard two women in the restroom talking about a man named Rex. She heard the intimacies she believed Rex was saying to her so sincerely coming from another woman's lips.

Thelma stormed out of the restroom and found Rex. After he recovered from the shock, Thelma informed him, "You were the topic of the conversation in the ladies' room."

"Really?" he said, for I'm sure he could think of nothing else, his face reddening even in the dim lights of the dance club.

Thelma told me, "You know, Donna, if I had slept with Rex, this incident would have crushed and humiliated me. Thank God, He did not let that happen."

Thelma realized, too, establishing a pattern of sleeping with men increased her odds of walking into a singles' gathering to face several men who knew her naked body. As bad as that thought is, worse still is her conscience, the inner voice, telling her how wrong it is that several men know her in the biblical way.

I watch this happen to many of my single friends, I see their reputations plunge, and I see the good men increasingly leave them alone.

"The way it turned out," Thelma continued, "I felt confident and cheerful. I walked away with my self-respect. I could laugh at his discomfort. He looked foolish, not me. Now I know what you said in your book is true."

She got it. God wants her to be happy.

Chapter 3

Why Want a Man, Anyway?

You know the cliché, "You can't live with them and you can't live without them"? It makes me feel like shouting affirmatively, "Amen. This is truth."

Every time my single women friends get together, the topic of conversation is men. Yes, men — every single time we get together.

We are constantly trying to figure them out. We are constantly trying to learn what we need to do to get the one we want and keep him. We ask ourselves:

Where is he?

How do I meet him?

Will he like me?

What should I say?

How do I indicate my interest?

Should I ask him to dance?

Should I call him if he doesn't call me?

Usually I just listen because I've chosen not to date much. Like a lot of women, I refuse to date anyone who will not ask me out first. I will encourage him so he will know I am interested, but I will not ask him out.

In fact, look around. Used to be women would date just about anyone simply to have a date on Saturday night.

No longer. Women have become highly discriminating. We choose to go out alone or stay home rather than be saddled with an unsatisfactory date all evening long.

Why?

Sex.

Sex has really caused a major upheaval in dating practices.

Sex has caused more rejection for men . . . and you know how men hate rejection.

Women know — to date is to be pressured for sex. If a woman is not immediately interested, she will not take the chance of accepting a date. Thus, a man is not given much of a chance for a woman to get to know his many wonderful qualities.

A woman can no longer assume she will be able to date a man for long without sexual expectations. And no longer is public opinion in her court.

Consequently, women will not go out with anyone with whom they cannot see themselves making love. Most respectable women are not into sport sex. So, we have many free nights.

Many a man feels rejected for this reason. The more often he feels rejected, the fewer times he will ask out a woman.

Do you see the vicious circle?

We are at an impasse.

Nobody wins.

How can dating become a win-win experience again?

* * *

As a woman you do want a man in your life. You may profess otherwise because of the experiences you have had dating. But deep down you want that romance. You want the caring, the sharing, the caressing, the loving only a man can supply. After all, God created us this way.

Many of you have declared you do not want a man. You say you are happy just the way you are. Many of you attempt to convince yourselves and everyone around you of your independence. Some of you have actually succeeded in convincing yourself, if not others. I know — I was once one of you.

But when questioned, upon hearing a description of an ideal relationship, each of you agree you would be happier in such a scenario.

Meanwhile we ask ourselves:

Why do we want a man?

What is it about a relationship that I feel I need?

Am I not satisfied with my women friends?

Am I not satisfied with my relationship with my God?

What is God's plan?

What is God's Plan?

From Genesis through Revelation, God's plan is for man and woman to abide together. God created us this way. That's why craving someone to love and to love us in return is universal and normal.

Sex is intimacy and displays love. Sex demands a connection between a man and a woman. Perhaps sex is God's way of requiring us to care for each other, of demanding love.

Apart from the affection and caring sex provides and which we miss as single women, extremely practical reasons exist why God wants man and woman together. God ordained the family uniting Adam and Eve after forming Eve out of Adam's side especially for a helpmate. That was his perfect plan. And since the fall in the Garden of Eden, man continues to mess things up.

God allows me to ask the silliest questions — like when Eve ate of the fruit of the tree of Knowledge of Good and Evil, what would have been the outcome if Adam refused her tempting offer? Adam got blamed, not Eve.

When I feel inadequate to handle my position as head of a household, a single working mother, I remind myself of God's perfect plan.

It also occurred to me the flesh first emerged as a life force when the serpent got involved. He offered instant gratification. The woman saw the fruit of the tree, that it was good fruit and pleasing to the eye, and also desirable for gaining wisdom, so she ate. She apparently did not consider long-range consequences.

She wanted instant satisfaction to appease the flesh.

After Eve listened to the serpent and ate the fruit, she came under the spell of lust and greed and idolizing wisdom, placing knowledge above her faith in God. So it became obvious to me, a practical and logical woman, if we lust after something, a chance exists that flesh will rule our lives. If we allow our flesh to rule, we do not allow the Spirit to reign.

Can't you just imagine what Adam was thinking?

"What's going on here?" he probably wondered. "I don't want to create trouble with Eve. I love her. Man, she'll probably kick me out of bed tonight if I don't eat this blasted fruit."

Of course, we don't know whether or not Adam and Eve were enjoying sex at this point, but fellowship was certainly important. Fellowship is important to God because it is why He created us in the first place.

Adam, probably afraid of Eve withdrawing her fellowship, agreed to do the one thing God told him specifically not to do. Eve obviously wielded enough influence to persuade Adam to go against God.

Disagreements likely never arose between them in the garden before the serpent's arrival, so Adam did not know how to handle the situation.

Well, this is awful, Adam possibly thought, *but lately I'm with Eve a whole lot more than I'm with God. So I'll compromise on this one little thing. God won't mind.*

It is probable everything had come easily to the happy couple and now dealing with the stress the serpent brought into their lives was new to them. Adam and Eve probably felt they did not need God if they figured things out themselves. Knowledge is what the serpent promised them. What better way to figure things out than to possess God's own knowledge?

Adam and Eve reasoned, rationalized, justified, and ate. Nothing's changed.

Do you remember what happened after Adam ate the fruit? Here comes God, walking in the Garden in the cool of the evening. He knew exactly what happened, but did He make any accusations? No! He simply asked them, "Where are you?" He knew where they were and what they did, but He wanted them to admit their wrong. God wants us to confess so we will know what we did wrong.

Perhaps overcoming sins is why, when dining with the disciples after his resurrection, Jesus asked Peter three times, "Peter, do you love me? Then feed my lambs" (John 21:15-17). Was this the way Jesus pardoned Peter for the three times Peter denied Him? Jesus gave Peter three opportunities to confirm his love. Three denials. Three confirmations. Did these confirmations overcome the sins of denial? We'll know when we get to heaven.

Adam uttered the first confession of fear when he said to the Lord, "I heard you in the garden, and I was afraid because I was naked; so I hid" (Gen. 3:10). Fear surfaced when man's flesh started ruling over the spirit.

After the fall of man, *then and only then* did God place woman in a position of submission, her husband ordained to rule (Gen. 3:16). God's perfect plan was for us to walk side by side. Now His permissive plan is our submission for our protection. Look what woman did when she enjoyed equal billing. And she did not even receive blame.

I don't know about you, but when I feel inadequate, knowing God planned for my protection is a relief to this weaker vessel.

What does the Bible say on the subject of men and women together? Many Scriptures discuss the subject.

Best known are Genesis 2:18: "It is not good for the man to be alone," and Proverbs 18:22: "He who finds a wife finds what is good and receives favor from the Lord." First Corinthians 11:11, written by Paul says, "In the Lord, however, woman is not independent of man, nor is man independent of woman."

This is God's plan. Men and women need each other.

The main reason I want a man?

I want God's best.

Help! This Is Not What I Planned!

Recalling my upbringing, at times I am furious. Dad lied to me. He did not mean to, but he lied to me. Dad told me I would marry and produce children. He said some man would protect and care for me for life. Most women received the same message. Our brothers needed financing for college. Women did not. This attitude is historical — until now. Just my luck.

Women of my generation believed we would marry, stay home, and raise children. The possibility of managing a household and all of its problems alone never occurred to me. Nor did the idea of working the rest of my life.

As a mother of a daughter myself, I do my best to guide her preparation for the future. Observing her friends, however, they want the same things out of life we wanted. They want to marry and stay married, but they know the odds.

Many young women are from fractured families and do not want to suffer the way their divorced mothers suffered financially. Yet if a career keeps them away from their families, they do not want that either. Their own mothers were not around when they were needed, and these future moms want better for their own children.

Single women raising children alone make up a major segment of our family units today. In fact, as of 1989 there were 10,890,000 families with a mother raising children under 18 alone. This is only those families with children under 18. The baby boomers, like me, have children in college and over 18. This would add millions more to the number of families. Of the 10,890,000 families, 42.8 percent of the families are living below the poverty level, and 4.8 million women are due child support. In fact, 53 percent of all children living with their mothers are living below the poverty level compared to only 10 percent of those living with both parents.

Think about it. With nearly half the number of families under the poverty level and with each family representing at least one other person, that represents more than 10,000,000 individuals our government must find a way to help financially. And this does not include those families with children in college who also need financial help.

There are 92,830,000 family units. The ten million figure above represents 11.7 percent of the American households. Including baby boomers with college-age children, I would guess the figure of single-parent homes headed by women would be closer to 15 percent of the current family units. The figure of 11.7 percent is an increase from 1970. That year 5,500,000 homes were headed by women, or 8.7 percent.

Married families in 1989 numbered 52,100,000 and represented 56.1 percent. This figure is down considerably since 1970. During 1970 there were 44,728,000 homes with both parents, or 70.0 percent. We can only guess what the difference has been since 1960 or 1950.

Those households headed by single males in 1989 numbered 2,847,000 or 3.1 percent. This figure is up since 1970 when 1,228,000 households or 1.9 percent of the homes were headed by single men.[2]

These figures do not take into account the huge number of women who have remarried, but did live with this issue for a time between marriages. These statistics do not consider the 15,120,000 females who are widowed, divorced, or single and living alone. They, too, must deal with sexual issues today.

This is not God's plan.

Women individually face trials never before experienced by so many.

Nationally, we feel the aftermath in our pocketbook with massive welfare systems to handle the responsibilities so many men left behind. Sex is not a private issue. With one and a half million legal abortions each year, with 12 million cases of sexually transmitted diseases, with generational existence of unwed mothers on public assistance . . . to say that sex is a private issue is ludicrous.

In his seminar "Marriage Plus," Ray Mossholder gives statistics that 20 men left their wives for every 1 woman who left her husband in 1970. Today two women leave their husbands for every one man who leaves his wife.

Men now recognize it is not as fun being single as they thought it would be when they left their families in droves. Many divorced men now acknowledge a different partner every night gets old fast. Having *one* someone love them was better. Recent studies show married men are the happiest people. Figuring the male happiness factor in a marriage on a scale of 1 to 7, with 7 being high — 45.6 percent rate their marriage a 7; 30.7 percent rate their marriage a 6; and 11.7 percent rate it a 5.

In other words, 88 percent of the men rate their marriage above average.

As for satisfaction with family life, 84 percent rated themselves a "very great deal" satisfied, "great deal" satisfied, or "quite a bit" satisfied. Another 9 percent rated their satisfaction "a fair amount." In other words, 93 percent were satisfied being married. That means only 7 percent were not satisfied in their marriages.

* * *

James tells us to "consider it joy" when we face diverse trials. "Consider it pure joy, my brothers, whenever you face trials of many kinds, because you know that the testing of your faith develops perseverance" (James 1:3). In the original language this Scripture actually can translate "throw a party." Believe me, it is extraordinarily difficult to throw a party when in the midst of the trials of being a single parent.

As a single parent, you worry about where to live, who will take care of your children while you work, and where your next meal will come from. You ponder how to get your children to and from events during office hours, how to pay their dental and health related expenses, and who will watch the children when they are ill. You upset yourself over how to pay for school needs. How will you provide a college education? How will you provide yourself with a car that runs and eventually your teens with transportation? How do you take the car in for repairs and get to and from the office? And on and on and on.

Single parents face these issues, and scores more, with no other adult to lighten the load.

Only another single parent understands the isolation and the fear of going it alone.

Raised in a single-parent household by my father, I quickly realized how relatives and friends rallied around my father. I noticed, too, how my father did not offer to help me when I divorced. Why?

Raising children is not the normal role for a father. Grandma and Grandpa and aunts and uncles rushed to Dad's rescue. Although today fathers head more single parent households, my research shows it is still more difficult for the single working mother.

Possible reasons are listed below.

Setting Policy

The opportunities to set company policy or make demands does not exist for most women. Most women do not reach positions to influence such decisions. Women achieve middle management and receive token board appointments (88 percent of all board members are white males), but remain shunned by Mahogany Row — that floor in every corporation where the highest executives are located, traditionally allocated to persons of the masculine gender. Any woman lucky enough to be on Mahogany Row will normally have a desk located just outside an executive's office.

Recent statistics show white males occupy 97 percent of the upper management positions. Only 42 percent of the work force are white males while 39 percent are white females. This means 42 percent of the working population makes 97 percent of the decisions. Or conversely, 39 percent of the working population makes only 3 percent of the decisions. A minority whip with a 3 percent backing would not enjoy much control or influence.

Why the huge discrepancy? Is it because men do not see the benefits if women obtained these positions? What a shame. It is possible we could realize huge savings in taxes which finance the welfare system and soon the health system.

Unfortunately, the result of this inequality is that white males decide policy and procedure. With wives and paid staff assisting these men, they do not understand the issues of the single working parent. According to the Department of Labor, Women's Division, 70 percent of all women between the ages of 24 and 54 are in the work force. The problem will only get worse before it gets better.

Financial Position

The single working mom usually is not in the financial

position to hire needed help. The *Statistical Abstract of the U.S.* shows in 1987 working women earned 50 cents for each dollar working men earned. This is up from 41 cents on the dollar in 1970. Full-time working women made 67 cents on the dollar in 1988, up from 60 cents on the dollar in 1980. It is an improvement, but not what it should be.

As mentioned before, 42.8 percent of working mothers are below the poverty level. What if 42.8 percent of the population was below the poverty level? If it were men who suffered these injustices, something would quickly be done about it.

Single women also lack finances because of the millions of "deadbeat dads" who don't pay child support. Again, 4.8 million families headed by women are due back child support. Considering there are 10,890,000 households, this computes to 44.1 percent. And I wonder how many, like me, never reported their husband's lack of payment. This figure could be even higher. Sad!

Responsibilities

Much of the blame for the single working mother not getting ahead lies in her responsibility for the children. She cannot dedicate the hours required to climb the corporate ladder.

As a recruiter (my profession), one of the engineers I have placed in the past is a single woman. Janice has two children under the age of 12. Recently she called me to get her out of the major corporation where I placed her. She is being passed over for promotions. Janice has to arrange for the move of her family alone. She cannot just drop everything and move, leaving the arrangements to someone else as the men can. Consequently, she is not getting ahead.

Dan's situation is a perfect example of the flip side of this dilemma. Dan is a former police chief of a small town in Texas. He left his job when he and his wife divorced. Since that time, he had difficulty finding the right job.

Finally, Dan found a position on the Tulsa police force, with promotional opportunities into arson investigation, his expertise. Rapidly promoted to the Tulsa arson team, Dan was offered an opportunity for further advancement.

Soon after Dan found the position in Tulsa, his ex-wife died leaving him the responsibility of their two children. When offered the second advancement, Dan knew the position required more hours in the field and more hours traveling, as well as a relocation to Oklahoma City. Not wanting to leave his children alone when they had so recently lost their mother, he was forced to refuse the job.

Dan now finds his career limited.

Amazing how sympathetic Dan is now about the issues facing working parents.

* * *

The problems women face this century differ vastly from past problems. In ancient biblical times when something happened to a husband, the wife and her children returned to her family. Sadly, few single women appear in the Bible, but we can examine several.

Elijah and the Widow

The Lord sent Elijah to the widow when she was about to prepare her last meal. Elijah told her, "Don't be afraid. Go home and do as you have said. But first make a small cake of bread for me from what you have and bring it to me, and then make something for yourself and your son. For this is what the Lord, the God of Israel, says: 'The jar of flour will not be used up and the jug of oil will not run dry until the day the Lord gives rain on the land' " (1 Kings 13-14).

Can you imagine?

Envision preparing your last meal. At the end of your rope mentally and financially, along comes a prophet asking you to serve him. And he wants the last food you have left in the world.

What a joyful surprise it must have been. With the words of his mouth, this prophet speaks and your needs supernaturally materialize.

Elijah moved in with the widow for three years (1 Kings 18:1). I'm sure she was thrilled with Elijah's help. She certainly needed it until her son matured enough to act as man of the house. The widow trusted Elijah and they both trusted God, and her life-or-death circumstances disappeared.

Elisha and the Widow

Another widow is the wife of a man from a company of prophets.

> She cried out to Elisha, "Your servant my husband is dead, and you know that he revered the Lord. But now his creditor is coming to take my two boys as his slaves.
> Elisha replied to her, "How can I help you? Tell me, what do you have in your house?"
> "Your servant has nothing there at all," she said, "except a little oil" (2 Kings 4:1-2).

Elisha told her exactly what to do. Supernaturally, Elisha supplied the widow's needs with his words, and she went into the oil business (2 Kings 4:3-7). She asked a man for advice, a man who trusted God.

Naomi, Ruth, and Boaz

In the Book of Ruth, Naomi's husband, Elimelech, died and left with her two sons, Mahlon and Kilion. Her sons probably cared for Naomi as much as she cared for them, sharing responsibilities of the household. Her sons later married Moabite women, Orpah and Ruth.

Ten years later, both sons died. Alone in a household with her two daughters-in-law, with no way to support the family, what was Naomi going to do?

Traveling on the road to Judah returning to her family, Naomi told her daughters-in-law to go to their home. She also asked that God grant that each of them would "find rest in the home of another husband."

Orpah kissed Naomi goodbye and returned to her family. Ruth clung to Naomi, and spoke these famous words: "Where you go I will go, and where you stay I will stay. Your people will be my people and your God my God. Where you die I will die, and there I will be buried. May the Lord deal with me, be it ever so severely, if anything but death separates you and me."

Talk about loyalty! Ruth recognized the power of God in Naomi and in her family.

To earn her keep, Ruth gleaned ears of corn from fields of Boaz, a relative of Naomi's husband, Elimelech. Shortly, Ruth became a servant, unusual for a foreigner, and a highly coveted position. This is the second matchmaking noted in the Bible, the first being Isaac's wife, Rebekah (Gen. 24:12-66).

Naomi tells Ruth to wash and perfume herself. Naomi instructs Ruth to lay at the end of the bed while Boaz sleeps after a night of drink and good spirits. This was a sign she wanted him to assume responsibility for her as a "kinsman-redeemer" (Ruth 1:1-3:4). Today this same action is an open invitation and not advisable. Was it then, too?

Boaz and Ruth married, and became ancestors of our Lord Jesus Christ.

John, Jesus, and Mary

Jesus on the cross directed John to take Mary into his own home. He directed John to treat Mary as he would his own mother (John 19:27). Then the end came.

* * *

History shows women treated in much the same manner.

For example, reading an historical Civil War novel, I noticed the woman of the house had complete responsibility for managing the home. She managed servants, if any, supervised purchasing, delivery, maintenance, and all activity regarding the interior of the house. She did all of this, plus raised and nurtured the children. Her job, a major responsibility, was a full-time position inside the home.

Men frowned on a woman in business, though it was not unheard of. If a lady inherited an estate, then opportunity existed for her to take on the responsibilities if she so desired. The downside? A business woman attracted few men. Also, she added to her trials the aggravation of people taking advantage of her naiveté in business.

Attitudes have changed little in some ways, but they have changed vastly in others.

Someone recently asked our singles' Sunday school how many ever expected to attend a singles' Sunday school class. How did my generation get so lucky? Why suddenly do women face more difficulties alone than ever before in history?

My plans included protection and care from a loving husband. My plans included a family tree showing the perfect family chain with no erasures or white-outs. My plans included celebrating a fiftieth anniversary. My plans included a family burial plot. How did the family end up on the list of endangered species?

I admit it. I never dreamed I would attend a singles' Sunday school class. This is not what I planned.

Needless to say, I feel unprepared to handle my present situation.

Where do I go for help?

Business Help?

For all our sophistication, the business world is not much different today. There is a "good-ole-boy network," but where is the network for "good-ole-girls"?

Women in the business world compete with other women for the attention of the men in management to get promotions. This competition is the same competition women experience in their search to find a husband.

Few, if any, women understand the mentor system, that the "hand-up" to the next woman will actually help long-range.

Women who work face problems we can handle only during working hours, and there is no one else to do it. Many of the problems we face we receive no training or information on how to handle. Where can we go for guidance we need in business or with our automobiles or with our investments or major purchases? In all of these areas women rarely receive instruction.

We did not receive instruction from our mothers, because our mothers did not know any of this. We did not receive instruction or training from our fathers because they had no idea we might need it.

If you start talking to me about retirement or investments, I freeze up. I don't understand it. I don't want to understand it.

I've got enough on my plate without that to worry about, yet I probably should make it a concern.

Can I hire someone to help me? I probably can't afford to.

Can I trust a salesman? Odds are they want to sell me something.

Where do I go for help I can afford?

Another business concern? Taking care of a car. There ought to be a network to protect us.

When I worked for a major temporary help firm in the city, I was shocked to discover the differences women were forced to pay for equal services. From time to time we would get orders from the major automobile manufacturers for "secret shoppers." Driving a certain type of automobile, a man and a woman each would drive into a dealership, and ask the price of a specific service and part, such as replacing a faulty starter. The differences in price in favor of the male customer was close to half what the woman was charged. Hopefully, things have changed since then, but how would we know?

Also included in the area of business concerns would be household repairs and expenses.

Recently a television magazine show set up repairmen to see how honest they were. They arranged something as simple as a piece of plastic falling down in the dishwasher causing a malfunction. One repairman out of eight was honest, explained exactly what had happened, and charged only for the trip. Seven others came up with false repairs. Had something as simple happened at home to a woman, she would have been forced to call a repairman. Many men would have been able to look at the dishwasher and discover the malfunction without ever calling a repairman.

Consequently, men do not know how much work it is to handle alone a house with even one child when you are so completely ill-prepared.

Men in management apparently do not understand if a parent must leave work during the day. In fact, the parent will probably get pay docked, and it could eventually lead to termination. Although it is changing a bit, we're still a long way from solving the issue.

Women usually would do better with the advice of a man in business affairs.

Having a husband is still God's best plan.

Family Help?

You might think a single-parent mom could go to her parents for help. Not likely. Most parents never faced divorce. The next generation will not be able to say the same. Our parents do not know the demands. They cannot relate. Even for those of us raised in single-parent homes, some reason may exist for a lack of understanding.

My own parents divorced in the early sixties when divorce was still considered disgraceful. In 1959, according to the *1961 World Almanac,* there were 183,421 divorces. And that was an increase of 7.5 percent over 1958.

According to the *1994 World Almanac* there were 292,000 divorces the first quarter of 1993. And this was a decrease from 4.9 per 1,000 population to 4.6 per thousand population. For 12 months there were 1,206,000 divorces. That computes from 1959 until now to a 658 percent increase in the number of divorces per year.

No wonder our parents do not understand.

What happened?

As I said, my parents were different, divorcing in 1961. They prearranged, in the event of divorce, that my two brothers and I would live with Dad. As earlier mentioned, it was amazing how many relatives and friends rushed to my father's assistance.

Dad was a managing engineer with a managing engineer's salary. Yet, knowing the difficulties of a single parent, Dad rarely offered to help me. Dad made the token verbal offers to babysit, but every time I called to ask him (and I seldom called), he was busy. I recall five times he actually did watch his granddaughter. I assume Dad's reasoning was that as a woman I could handle it.

I was thrilled when I found facts to back up my conviction. According to a survey, in regard to transportation issues, single men have help from others 59 percent of the time compared to single women at 56 percent of the time. Of this figure, 41 percent of the men receive help from their parents while only 11 percent of the women have the same help. I wonder how much the women had to pay?

In regard to repairs, single men have help 52 percent of the time, while women receive help only 23 percent of the time. Of this figure, 48 percent of the men received help from their parents, while only 7 percent of the women received such help. I wonder how much women paid?

In regard to housework, 52 percent of the men received help from their parents, while only 16 percent of the women received such assistance.[3]

Do these figures seem lopsided to you?

Another reason going to her family is difficult for today's woman is the mobile family. Many a divorced mom lives in a community hundreds of miles away from any family and friends.

Reviewing history, we find larger and more complex family structures including dynasties, tribes, clans, houses, and village communities. Several generations lived and worked together. Ancestors inspired distant ancestors for generations to come, customs were perpetuated through centuries, and religions were deeply rooted. Family members provided a source and a refuge for their own homeless and needy. Thousands of years of society have enjoyed this stable bond.

Today this bond is so slack it provides no support and no stability. The family is disintegrating. We have been stripped down to the simplest form of familial expression.

Television talk shows report about older children living at home. Until recent generations this has been normal operating procedure for the family. Only recently we have found it odd.

Again, having a husband is still God's best plan.

Spiritual Help?

Where does the single parent go for spiritual help and for that prayer of agreement?

Most Christians agree it is ideal to go for prayer to someone you know and who knows you. Ideally, this person knows your problems, and can relate. This person, hopefully, is someone you respect enough to allow yourself to become accountable.

How frustrating it is to explain your situation to a different person each time you need prayer. A telephone prayer line is impersonal. They don't know you. They don't know your situation. Don't misunderstand, I have answered the prayer line at my church and I know we do wonderful work for those who call. A prayer line will never take the place of a close personal relationship with a prayer partner.

Do single mothers go to other friends with prayer needs?

Married friends, busy with their own families and their own tight schedules, rarely enjoy surplus time. Moreover, by virtue of their marital status they need not step outside their own home to find a partner for prayer.

Unmarried friends deal with the same problems, the same tight schedules, the same lack of finances. They find it difficult carrying their own burdens, much less worrying about another's. Also, if a prayer partner's problems appear equally overwhelming, Satan will try to dupe you into believing the Bible does not work.

Furthermore, would these friends experiencing the same trials likely be able to instruct someone else with the same prayer needs?

"This was exactly my situation today," Angela said when I told her about this section of the book. "I wanted someone I could call to pray with. I wanted some serious advice. But my problem is that I don't know anyone who isn't dealing with the same problems and having the same results."

Angela is a well-read and highly educated woman who supports her daughter alone. She has spent a great deal of time in her Bible, much time attending a Bible institute, much time teaching the Bible to others, and much time counseling.

"The Lord has led me through many Red Sea experiences," Angela continued. "You would think I would become accustomed to them. Each one is unique. Each one different. Frankly, I just want to spend some time with someone I know has been through what I have been through. I want a spiritual mentor for a prayer partner. Is that possible?"

Ideally, we could all find a prayer partner a step or two higher in spiritual position to exhort and encourage us. In turn, we could be a blessing to another lower spiritually to exhort and encourage them. Sort of a spiritual mentor system.

The next best thing to a personal prayer partner is a Bible fellowship or study group, but it's just not the same.

Where else can we go for help? To the church? Doubtful. Observations indicate pastors often publicly pray for marriage restoration, but seldom for the needs of singles. Many churches support singles' ministries, yet married couples govern these ministries, usually young married couples.

Everywhere singles turn, the same story. Yet God wants us to look out for the orphans and the widows in their distress. "Religion that God our Father accepts as pure and faultless is this: to look after orphans and widows in their distress" (James 1:27). Are not single moms the widows of this century? Are single moms not the fastest growing poverty group in the nation?

Individually, you might be able to kindle a change in your own church.

For example, I attended one of the fastest growing churches in the country with nearly 10,000 present for services each week. Even as large as this church is, the pastor cares for the individual.

Responding to a five-page, single-spaced letter written about singles, within two weeks our pastor gave a sermon addressing single parents. When he asked singles in the audience to stand, the "guesstimates" on the percentage standing ranged from 40 percent to 75 percent.

In his sermon, our pastor stated indicators that show the number of single-parent homes will exceed dual-parent homes by the year 2000. We are a major segment of the population and we will soon receive the notice we deserve.

Are all pastors responsive? Are you dealing with a similar situation in your church? Are your needs disregarded?

It's sometimes better to do anything than to do nothing. Why not write your pastor? You can make a difference, not selfishly, but for every single in your church.

The very day the pastor received my letter (a Wednesday) he prayed for single parents at the end of the service that night. When asked, hundreds of singles stood for prayer.

The pastor asked for testimonies and one lady came forward to report she forced herself to come that night. She said the prayer for single parents ministered to a particular need. She believed the word she received was the reason Satan tried to keep her away. God meant for her to hear the pastor's words.

Hearing her testimony, the pastor felt led to spend another ten minutes ministering to singles. It was a letter he read that very afternoon which prompted this teaching.

One person can make a difference and you can be that person in your home church. Would not the possible result be worth the effort?

Still the church may not be the place to get spiritual help for a single person. Married people just do not understand. The same pastor above, who has always been married, caused some major problems recently for a single friend.

Al, a former drug addict and alcoholic, is now an ordained pastor with over ten years of sobriety who is twice divorced. His ex-wives re-married years ago. Al gave his life to Christ when the last wife left. A counselor at our church, Al volunteers his services, free of charge, his only purpose to disciple others.

Al is a "man's man," but the women love him, too. He stands ramrod straight, as though he had a steel backbone. Ham-sized hands are constantly in use holding another's hand in prayer. His nearly bald head, sprinkled with blonde hairs, is easily recognized in any crowd. When he preaches, his former heathen toughness shows through, but when his blue eyes sparkle, the truth of what he teaches is obvious.

Recently he met someone. They began dating. His friend, Becky, is also divorced.

I do not understand all the circumstances, but apparently the pastor, who preaches love, called Al and Becky into his office for a confrontation. The pastor wanted them to stop dating. Pastor did not want Al dating a divorced woman.

Al looked the pastor in the eye and said, "If that is what you believe, then everything you have said out there in the pulpit is a lie."

The pastor explained that Becky was not free to remarry. Becky told the pastor, "I don't know if it will be Al or someone else with whom I spend the rest of my life, but I assure you, it will not be my ex-husband."

Al left the church.

Is that what the pastor wanted? I doubt it.

Little sense is made of the argument that God will kick His kids out of heaven because they decide to remarry after divorce. Is He going to love us less when we fail as His children than when we fail as sinners? Not likely.

Why did the pastor feel he could involve himself so much in the life of a volunteer for the church? Sure, he could have removed him from service if he felt something was amiss, but this appears to me to be overstepping the bounds. Yes, we are, as Christians, to be submitted to others, but not to our church in a manner that controls our family decisions. Then it becomes too close to a sect, not simply a church.

Attitudes like this pastor's attitude cause singles to flee from churches all across this nation. Singles separate themselves from this type of spiritual help.

Of course, a change in church attitude does not resolve the issue of a prayer partner.

My survey of Christian women indicates many of us are "holding out" for someone capable of being the spiritual head of the household. Few women want someone they have to "bring along."

Having the right husband is still God's best plan.

Chapter 4

Thankful? For What?

With all our problems, we single moms can still count it all joy and throw a party, because of what Paul tells us. He says the widow (or single woman) who is really in need and left all alone puts her hope in God. "The widow who is really in need and left all alone puts her hope in God and continues night and day to pray and to ask God for help" (1 Tim. 5:5). If we are ignoring God He will allow the legs to be kicked right out from under us to compel us to turn to Him for help.

Personally, I know I would not be a Christian full of faith today if I had no difficulties and trials. These lessons are God's self-help program. When I had troubles I learned to trust God to fulfill His Word.

Examine your life. I am sure you can see the work of the Lord — definitely reason to throw a party. Thankfully, surrendering to God is the best situation to be in.

Recently, well-known athlete Meadowlark Lemon, renowned for his superhuman feats on the basketball court with the Harlem Globetrotters, spoke at our church. He said, "Once you ask Jesus into your heart, you can never turn back."

Discussing the sermon later, friends agreed this has certainly been true in our lives. Once Jesus abides in your heart, He is there for good. He will not let you slip for long before He yanks your chain to remind you who's in charge. He is the author and finisher of your faith. You cannot even take credit for that. He sets you back on the right path, making your path straight.

You no longer have a choice. You made your choice when you asked Jesus to take over. He, being a gentleman, accepted your invitation. He is there forever for your good. God has given us a gift. It is not something we earned or paid for. This gift is a new birth into a living hope brought to us via the resurrection of Jesus from the dead. We are given an inheritance that can never perish, spoil, or fade — kept in heaven for us (1 Pet. 1:4).

In this same Scripture we are told that we may suffer grief in all kinds of trials. But we are assured "These have come so that your faith — of greater worth than gold, which perishes even though refined by fire — may be proved genuine and may result in praise, glory and honor when Jesus Christ is revealed" (1 Pet. 1:7).

This inheritance is in heaven; it is the *"full inheritance."* Blessed here on earth, as in heaven, you come into your full inheritance when you reach your heavenly home. Like receiving interest off a trust fund before a certain age, you know you receive complete control of the trust when you turn the age set forth in the Last Will and Testament. You still receive interest now. You have special blessings now in this age.

One Scripture spoken by Jesus relates to this in particular:

> "I tell you the truth," Jesus replied, "no one who has left home or brothers or sisters or mother or father or children or fields for me and the gospel will fail to receive a hundred times as much *in this present age* (homes, brothers, sisters, mothers, children and fields — and with them, persecutions) and *in the age to come*, eternal life" (Mark 10:29-30;KJV, italics added).

Up to this point in this Scripture Jesus deals with relationships, but after this point He deals with material goods. Jesus is explicit. He says you will receive rewards here on earth, not just in heaven.

Persecutions come, but things left behind or lost for the gospel's sake, God returns a hundredfold. Until heaven, everything on earth is to show His work. In John 9:3 Jesus said, "This happened so that the work of God might be displayed."

God is in control and knows everything that is going to happen to you before it happens:

> O Lord, you have searched me and you know me. You know when I set and when I rise; you perceive my thoughts from afar. You discern my going out and my lying down; you are familiar with all my ways. Before a word is on my tongue you know it completely, O Lord (Ps. 139:1-4).

Trials come, but do the trials turn you to God? That is what He wants. Or do you let the trials turn you away from God?

Pat spoke recently at our church about her ten-year marriage to Joe. Three children came from the union. To everyone they appeared the perfect couple. In fact to Pat, they were the perfect couple.

Then Joe dumped her. Apparently Joe did not concur with prevailing opinion of their perfection status.

Pat was devastated. She couldn't believe God allowed this to happen.

Pat just knew God's will was for them to be together. She could quote Scripture and verse. Joe remarried quickly, but that did not deter Pat from praying that he leave number two and return to her. Pat could only see circumstances from her viewpoint, not God's viewpoint.

God did not answer Pat's prayers the way she wanted them answered. God answered later, in a much different way, exceeding her own dreams and desires.

Depressed, Pat played her piano and sang praise songs for hours on end to bolster her wavering spirit. She used to pray, "Lord, Your Word says that if I delight in You, You will give me the desire of my heart, which is. . . ." Pat always filled in the blanks for God. Amazing, is it not, how you cannot manipulate God?

Pat is now content and married to husband number three. This time she married a man who has since become an ordained minister. Together, they serve the Lord and co-pastor a church in Iowa. God is using Pat in ways she never dreamed possible.

None of this would have come to pass had she stayed with husband number one or husband number two. God allowed messes in her life to become messages.

Trials and problems are good for us to learn patience. And patience develops strength of character. It helps us to trust God more and more until we are strong in our faith, afraid of nothing.

> We also rejoice in our sufferings, because we know that suffering produces perseverance; perseverance, character; and character, hope. And hope does not disappoint us, because God has poured out his love into our hearts by the Holy Spirit, whom he has given us (Rom. 5:3-5).

You can go somewhere for help. Even if you do not attend a church, you can go somewhere. You can go to your Bible.

That is exactly what I did for years before I joined a church. I spent every night devouring the Word, learning and growing in knowledge. What I learned has been the most profound self-help odyssey because of God's supernatural power. Every other self-help program I tried was useless, probably because it relied on me and my power, not God's. Only learning what the Word says and relying on God has helped me.

Sadly, I bet not even a quarter of the Christian women I know have ever read their Bible from cover to cover. A much smaller number know their Bible well. Weekly these women listen to the pastor discuss one minuscule section of the Bible. Probably this is the extent of their contact with the Word of God for the rest of the week.

If you want to see God's miracle working power, perhaps you should rethink Bible reading. After all, our faith comes by hearing, and hearing by the Word of God. "Consequently, faith comes from hearing the message, and the message is heard through the word of Christ" (Rom. 10:17).

Without the knowledge imparted from the Bible, our manufacturer's handbook, you probably suffer needlessly alone. Remember the song "What a Friend We Have In Jesus"? It goes like this: "Oh, what peace we often forfeit. Oh, what needless pain we bear. All because we do not carry, everything to God in prayer."

As a single-again woman you were thrust into this lifestyle for which you probably received no preparation. Don't forfeit your peace. Don't needlessly bear the pain alone. Carry things to God in prayer. With the Bible, you have the help you need.

Can you count it all joy? How?

If you learn to turn to God.

The peace and joy you eventually experience is reason to be thankful.

* * *

Obviously, many very practical and extremely important reasons exist why God's plan is to respect a man in your lives. Even so, if you use your time wisely, turning to God and learning from Him, you can thank Him for this time alone.

Okay, God, we are thankful for the tribulation and the hard times, but we still want a man.

Having a husband, the right husband, is still God's plan.

Chapter 5

Greatest Joy — Greatest Challenge

The right relationship potentially can produce your greatest joy. Yet, establishing that relationship can be the most difficult task you face.

A major factor is you. Success in a relationship is not just finding the right person, it is also *being* the right person. The question is, how do we go about being a right person?

Obviously, it is not just for help that we women want a man in our lives, otherwise more women would marry.

Many women today prefer single status rather than married. With all the problems single moms face, it's understandable we want someone to help us with these needs. Here's the irony. Being around a man on a full-time basis can be the very reason many women divorce.

It is hard to be the right person when overworked and loaded with burdens. It is more difficult still when feeling used and unappreciated.

I was not a Christian when I filed for divorce. Considering a divorce, I realized that my alcoholic husband was simply another burden I could no longer afford to keep. I could not rid myself of my child. And my husband's inability to provide for his own home meant I could not rid myself of my job. In fact, the only burden I could get rid of was my husband. Many of the women I know feel the same.

The burdens I carried with him, the wrong person, were even more challenging than the burdens I would face alone. Yet even knowing this to be true, it was difficult to see it that way. I still *felt* more secure with a man in my life than I *felt* alone. When the decision had to be made, it was a rational and logical decision, based on facts. Had the decision been based on emotions, I would have stayed with him.

After Steve left, I did not date for years. I did not want another man, another burden, in my life. As someone pointed out to me recently, when Charles demonstrated the marriage I had dreamed of all my life, I began to have hope. This loving relationship, one like I enjoyed those months with Charles, could easily be my greatest.

Ah, but there is a problem.

With Charles I ended up in bed.

Is that what I can expect? Is there no way to find someone and date them long enough to marry them without being faced with compromising my morals?

Being single means I am forced to confront the issue of sex. Even if I never want a man in my life again, I still must face the issue of sex.

With all the tough situations facing singles, the greatest is the challenge to abstain from sexual sin.

Abstinence is painful. As women alone again we face a life of loneliness. Naturally, we miss and crave the feel of arms around us, comforting and caressing us.

Personally, I crave the protection and love that is biblical and literally built into my nature by the Creator. My surveys confirm I am not alone. No matter how hard I try to suppress the yearnings, I cannot do it by sheer willpower.

The feeling of inadequacy in the role of breadwinner can easily lead to sexual sin.

The lack of human warmth can lead to fornication simply for intimacy, no matter how fleeting.

Everyone wants someone to care about and to care about them. As Viktor Frankle states in his book *Man's Search for Meaning:*

> A thought transfixed me. For the first time in my life I saw the truth as it is set into song by so many poets, proclaimed as the final wisdom by so many thinkers. *The truth — that love is the ultimate and highest goal to which man can aspire.* Then I grasped the meaning of the great secret that human poetry and human thought and belief have to impart: The salvation of man is through love and in love.
>
> The second greatest commandment is to "Love your neighbor as you would yourself" (Matt. 19:19; Luke 10:27).[4]

Frankle may not have been a Christian, but the laws are evidently written on his heart as the Bible asserts:

> The requirements of the law are written on their hearts, their consciences also bearing witness, and their thoughts now accusing, now even defending them (Rom. 2:15).

An honest woman would admit wanting romantic love. You want a committed relationship. Yet odds are, if your background includes one or two revolving door relationships, you fear commitment.

You want someone in your life, but the pain of breaking up is something you never want to endure again. You may even joke, as many of my friends do, that you will not ever divorce again. You'll take him on an Amazon float trip, prick his finger, and toss him overboard. No divorce, just a carefully planned accident. When you were in the midst of the divorce process you probably wished yourself dead, or him dead — preferably him.

If you married before you became a Christian I'm sure you feel some comfort from the knowledge that you did not leave a Christian marriage. Even if it was a Christian marriage, as a well-known divorced evangelist says, "God is the God of a second chance."

But about that second chance, how do you go about meeting someone? A major step is meeting someone. Otherwise, nothing happens. Your choices look limited:

> 1) You can venture into the world. This usually means singles' clubs and drinking, assuring you will face sexual temptation. When faced with temptation, if you choose to be celibate, you will soon be sitting home without any dates;
>
> 2) You can stay in your circle of friends, your church, your gym, or at home. You will soon have met every unattached male in your church and your circle of friends and the gym. Then where will you go? You may be forced to face the fact you could be forever alone;
>
> 3) You could give in to temptation, and engage in sexual intercourse. You may believe the sentiment of today's society that you must make love in order to be loved.

Quite a challenge!

As a single, you face sex on a daily, almost hourly, basis. All around you people live together. Having a "significant other" has become as socially acceptable as a wife or a husband. In fact, the insurance coverage of a significant other has been legitimized by most employers' insurance companies.

No longer is it a scandal to give birth to a baby out of wedlock. A positive step, though, is the way Christians now help pregnant women with alternatives to abortion and with forgiveness. But the way celebrities and others have such an "in-your-face" attitude about their "arrangements" is disgraceful. These arrangements result in children who must face the stigma of forever being a celebrities' illegitimate offspring. And thousands of easily influenced fans now find shacking up acceptable because their idols do it.

Television routinely broadcasts programs where tales tell

of people jumping from bed to bed without a thought, programs that glorify ungodliness. Movies advertised on television leave almost nothing to the imagination. All around "SEX" and "SIN" scream at you, and it's just plain agony to remain virtuous.

The toughest part of all this is: As an adult single, you know how enjoyable sex can be. You are not a teenager who does not know the fruit. You tasted the fruit, and it was good. Odds are you would enjoy it if led by your sin nature, if you allow yourself to indulge in the flesh. You know you would enjoy it because you have experience to back it up.

The first time you step outside your conscience you can count on it bothering you. If you do not follow your spirit, your conscience, probably you'll indulge again. The second time leads to a longing. The longing becomes a need, the need becomes a craving, and eventually the craving becomes an addiction. Then sexual sin has control over you.

You might successfully stuff your conscience until it becomes numb. When you stuff your conscience, you stuff the Holy Spirit within you. That's a terribly dangerous thing to do.

Using myself as an example, I know that when I have sex in my life, I want to have sex more often. When I do not have sex in my life, I can choose to do other things. Like having chocolate in the house . . . you're going to eat it. If you refuse to bring it around, you don't miss it.

I know you have heard arguments that women can be celibate, but men cannot. Not one woman wrote any portion of the Bible. Man was first to preach celibacy. He may not want you to believe it, but it can be done.

Good news!

Even with all the outside pressure, if ever you gave your heart to Jesus, a point will come when you follow your conscience. The "Holy Hound of Heaven," as the Holy Spirit has been called, working in you, speaking to you, and teaching you, leads you into all truth. God continues His work conforming you into the likeness of His Son: "For those God foreknew he also predestined to be conformed to the likeness of his Son, that he might be the firstborn among many brothers" (Rom. 8:29).

Again, having a husband is God's plan.

Chapter 6

Sex and Consequences!

Recently, Jack discussed with me a relationship he was in. Jack, a tall, balding, attractive man, does not see himself as the charmer he is. Over and over he pairs up with trashy women who look like Las Vegas showgirls, not women you would take home to Mama. The looks of the women well represent their morals. Almost as though he believed people consider him more virile with a sexpot on his arm, Jack parades these women around for all to admire.

Jack began dating Melinda. She was wholesome and fresh and radically different than his normal "hussy honey." Consequently, Jack concluded Melinda was not the right woman. Unfortunately, they were already intimate sexually.

Jack did not want to hurt her, but he wanted to break it off. Sex kept him around. Melinda was an instrument for Jack's pleasure, and Jack did not want to give up his pleasure.

Finally Jack told Melinda, but not until another woman came along. Melinda was heartbroken.

What if Melinda could do a "do-over"? Do you think she would "do-over" her relationship with Jack? When she once gave her body, it was impossible to take it back. If Melinda knew in the beginning Jack just wanted her for sexual entertainment, do you think she would have stayed out of his bed? Would she now have a broken heart?

I don't know.

I do know if she had refrained, Jack would have moved on, minimizing the connection. Obviously, the less the connection, the less the heartbreak.

Would it now be possible for Melinda and Jack to become good friends? Doubtful. Sex is part of the picture and they cannot erase it from memory. It will color any friendship they attempt to establish . . . and not for the best.

Melinda got herself into this mess. She set herself up for a broken heart.

The trouble is, if you break up after you become intimate, men do not care to remain friends. Aside from the broken heart, you also lose a friend. If you cared enough for this person you were willing to climb into bed with him, it means you enjoyed his friendship. Sadly, you probably will never get another chance to establish a friendship.

When friendships develop first, there is always a chance it could turn into love. Would you not prefer building a lasting love out of a friendship rather than trying to make a friendship out of lost love?

What are the consequences, other than a broken heart, of sex outside of marriage?

Consequence No. 1 — Emotional

What emotional consequences did Melinda face when the affair ended?

Turmoil best describes what she probably felt. It is a normal affair-ending emotion. She probably also felt confused, used, abused, useless, unlovable, unlovely, and a failure. These heart-rending consequences could affect all her relationships for the remainder of her life.

Is a little pleasure in the sack for a season worth the agony of this defeat?

No woman can convince me that she has not felt some of

these emotions after such a liaison. If there is such a woman, I would be willing to bet big bucks she is not a Christian.

If a woman is not affected, she has hardened her heart to the voice of her conscience. Sadly, ignoring the prompting of her spirit means she inadvertently united with the god of darkness, allowing him a foothold.

Recent studies confirm the issue of emotional ties. A new catch phrase is "soul ties." The basis is biblical. About sex, it says the "two become one flesh" (Gen. 2:24 and 1 Cor. 6:16). This explains the ripping apart you feel in your soul which occurs when a breakup occurs. It also explains why breaking up is hard to do . . . even if the relationship is toxic.

Something was mentioned recently on a talk show about a hormone called oxytocin. They were saying something about it being a chemical secreted by the pituitary gland of the woman. They inferred that this chemical caused a chemical bonding during the sex act. Oxytocin, I discovered, is a synthetic hormone used to induce contractions for delivery and/or for milk production. The natural chemical produced by the female body is called vasopressin. It would make sense that a drug that caused contractions of the uterus might, indeed, set up some sort of chemical bonding.

Is this the real "chemistry" between two people? Pheromones? Pheromones are chemical signals passed between different organisms of the same species. Is this why a woman feels the bonding that men do not?

The Bible tells us the flesh is something we must bring under control, and we are to marry if we cannot control our flesh. "But if they cannot control themselves, they should marry, for it is better to marry than to burn with passion" (1 Cor. 7:9).

So, if you are having indiscriminate sex with many partners, you are like a ship without a rudder. Multiple partners causes fracturing of the headship God ordained over you. Every man you sleep with has a part of you. Scary thought, isn't it?

For the man, this idea of soul ties means he is spiritually head over every woman he sleeps with. He feels fractured as well. One woman probably cannot satisfy a man who has had many women.

Spiritually speaking, unless you break those soul ties, establishing a right relationship will be impossible. The only way to regenerate spiritually for someone new is to sever the ties. Pray specifically and ask God to break the ties in Jesus's name. "Do not be anxious about anything, but in everything, by prayer and petition, with thanksgiving, present your requests to God. And the peace of God, which transcends all understanding, will guard your hearts and your minds in Christ Jesus" (Phil. 4:6-7).

Marriage and sex in marriage are serious business to God. So serious, in fact, that He created a method of cutting a blood covenant when a woman experiences her first sexual intercourse.

Medical studies regarding the hymen of the woman show it to be a useless bit of flesh filled with blood. Throughout history the breaking of the hymen indicates the cutting of the marriage covenant. Historically, blood covenants extend beyond death to following generations. Some cultures demand the display of the marriage sheet to confirm the covenant. God created woman with this membrane, yet there is no physical reason for it to be there. It is, however, a concrete sign of the seriousness God places on the act of sex.

The biggest trouble with having multiple sex partners is the lack of importance you tend to bestow on sex, which was meant to be so holy and beautiful. If you give sex little importance now outside of marriage, why would you give it any more importance in marriage? Why would you give marriage much importance?

When you build your life around multiple sex partners, you build your life around multiple tragedies. It has to be so. Every relationship has to come to an end, unless you make it permanent. When sex is taken lightly, you become accustomed to pain and suffering, possibly thinking nothing is forever. You are experienced at tragedy, and well primed for adultery and divorce.[5]

Is this the way to contentment? Will it bring you happiness?

Tim Stafford suggests a rewrite to an old saying:

First comes love and sex, then comes an end to
the relationship. (repeat three times)

If you get pregnant go back to the beginning.
Then comes marriage.
Make up your own ending.[6]

In an affair emotions swim at high tide. What happens at low tide when the man leaves? Obviously, the emotions are left in little pools, in the bowels of the ocean rocks, shattered, never to reform in exactly the same way again. What emotions are left are stuffed until you maintain an ever-present numbness, a deadening of your feelings. You are neither happy nor sad . . . simply numb.

Is that what makes you happy? Not!

Consequence No. 2 — Physical

Physical consequences are many. Deadly consequences are diseases of all kinds, but the issue is too big to discuss here. Suffice to say there are 12 million reported cases of sexually transmitted diseases each year.

Tragically, every physical consequence has accompanying emotional consequences. If you have a friend who has died of AIDS, you know how emotional the physical consequences can be. The trouble is they have no way of truly determining what causes AIDS to be passed from one person to another. Some people have no clue how they contracted the disease. Blood tests, we are told, are not conclusive. The disease could remain dormant and undetected by any tests. No one can say definitely.

Is laying down in bed with someone worth laying down your life?

Still, the most heart-wrenching and far-reaching physical repercussion of sex outside of marriage is the conception of a helpless baby. There are four major consequences to this.

1) If you marry because of pregnancy, one or the other of you will always feel blackmailed into the marriage. This will cause your marriage to be clouded with unresolved suspicions from day one. Did he marry you only because of the child? The emotions are feeling trapped and feeling hopeless.

With sexual liberation coming on the heels "The Pill," it is ironic that there are more unwanted pregnancies now than at any time in our history. In fact, records kept on teenagers show that one-third of all teenage girls will become pregnant at some time during their teen years. Approximately 80 percent of all teenagers have reported being "in love" and nearly as many have had sex. Of those who have experienced sex for the first time, only 6 percent stop again for more than a year after the first relationship. This, of course, means that they have other relationships rather speedily.

About half of these young girls expect to marry their most recent sexual partner, but few of them actually will. The boys report differently, with 82 percent reporting they would not marry their most recent partner.[7] Obviously the difference in the figures means they failed to tell their girlfriend of this fact.

Keep in mind these figures are only for teenagers. This does not consider those who might be in their twenties, thirties, or forties. Can you imagine what an unwanted pregnancy can do to a career? Things are better today for the woman who is pregnant without a husband, but only somewhat.

2) If you keep a baby out of wedlock, you contend with possibly raising the baby without financial help. With the figure above showing that many families headed by females are living below the poverty level, it is a tragedy in the making. How many of these children turn to crime? How many of these children take their lives? How many of these children will follow the steps of the role model in their own lives? Are they the beginning of a generational curse? You cannot get any more emotional than futility and inadequacy.

3) If you decide to have a baby adopted out, you live with the thought of your child living somewhere without you. Practically weekly on some talk show we find people reuniting with lost family members with varying degrees of success. The end product of losing your child to adoption is you are left alone with an emptiness, a loneliness for that missing offspring.

4) If you opt for abortion, you live the rest of your days with guilt for murdering your own child. The figures now show there have been 1.5 million abortions a year in recent years, for a total of approximately 20 million aborted children since it became legal.

Unfortunately, I admit to being one of these statistics. Before I became a Christian I bought into the idea that it was simply tissue I was removing. I was married at the time and used abortion as a form of birth control. My experience cannot be that different from others. As soon as the "procedure" was complete, I had a deep and relentless awareness of the murder I had just committed. Later, after seeing the movie *The Silent Scream*, I was appalled at what I had done.

Thank God, He has forgiven me. It took me a lot longer to forgive myself. And I wonder sometimes if I did not have to suffer because of that choice. Did I allow Satan a foothold? Did he destroy my marriage as a result of my lack of knowledge? Was my lack of knowledge because of rebelliousness?

I do know I would give anything now if the abortion procedure had been illegal because I would not have gone through with a crime. Since we cannot seem to change the law back now, perhaps we can change the law regarding the supply of realistic education.

When contending with the issue of abortion, if you choose to go through with it, you will feel damned, doomed, and overwhelming shame. Only God can forgive.

Is even one night in the sack worth it?

Consequence No. 3 — Relationships

What will your future relationships be like?

The more relationships you have that fail, the thicker the walls you build. You either retreat or you try and try again.

Mickey Rooney married seven times prior to his present wife, Jan Chamberlin, a singer he met through his son, Mickey Jr. Now Mickey is a born-again Christian, outspoken and devoted. He has been married to Jan since 1978. He kept trying and kept trying and kept trying.

Another friend did the opposite. Lynda married young and was married for many years before her husband dumped her for a younger model. Since then, she has had one affair. Sadly, she discovered he was also married. That was 12 years ago. She has not dated since. And if she does not date, what are the odds she will find someone to marry?

Many of us never love again as we loved the first time, never again with that unbridled devotion. From the first relationship on we tend to withhold something of ourselves. Only with God in the equation can we truly let go of our fears and let God.

Unconsciously, we tend to blame the second person in our life for the sins of the first, in effect punishing him for things he has not done. The same thing happens with the next and the next and the next. With each progressive person, we add a new suit of garbage-filled baggage.

Sharing your body with multiple lovers diminishes for you the significance of sex and relationships and marriage. You begin to feel this "throw-away" mentality as will many of the partners you encounter.

In his book *Sexual Chaos*, Tim Stafford devotes almost two whole pages specifically to the "sexually experienced." Part of what he says follows:

> But what about those who have lost count of their extramarital liaisons? What difference could one more make to a person who has known many? A virgin is different from a non-virgin. But how different is a man who has known five women from a man who has known six?
>
> The difference may not be in the number of past partners, *but in whether the man has stopped adding more — or has not stopped.* That would make, at any rate, a difference in his relationship with God. Those who continue to pursue unmarried sex decide not to honor God with their body.[8]

The question of sex outside of marriage is often put this way: "Why deprive them?" One must ask, "Deprive them of what? Of sex?" But of what kind of sex, if it is outside of marriage? Do we deprive them of sex as a compulsive need? Sex as an abuse of themselves and others? Sex as a depersonalized, short-term round of biological stimulation? Sex as an opportunity to make their bodies known to others, and then to have them compared and rejected?

When you crawl in bed with someone without benefit of a covenant, you are opening yourself up for hurt. Again. And again. And again.

I know . . . you feel pressured. You feel you must "put-out" in order to have a man in your life. So you place the blame on men. They, after all, are only after one thing.

But guess what! Men blame us. That's right, they blame us for being available. One man recently asked me what he was supposed to do? He said a woman would get mad if he did not make a pass. If he did do to her what she wanted, he felt pressure. Commitments were expected that were not going to be made.

If what he says is true, why are men always trying to get us in bed?

One of the arguments nearly every woman has heard from men is the question of sexual compatibility. You can argue, though, this does not worry you. You know whether or not you like sex. If you are like me and the women I surveyed, you love sex. I am fairly certain that I enjoy sex as much, if not more, than someone sexually active. I do not need to prove myself. I do not believe I need to worry about whether or not a man and I would be sexually compatible.

Besides, in an affair I am inhibited. Other women have told me they experience the same emotions. I cannot relax and really enjoy a sexual relationship with someone who is not committed to be there beyond midnight.

I fully expect, based on past experience, to work out any problems after marriage. In fact, I was discussing this subject recently with Scott, a gentleman friend. I asked him just exactly how many times he had had sex that was no good. He admitted he could only think of two times.

"That being true," I asked, "how does it follow that you won't be satisfied having sex with someone you love after you are married?"

You can tell if a man turns you on without committing a sin against God. Men, too, are quite capable of this pre-determination.

Recently I watched a talk show about virginity. A young

virgin in her late twenties, whom I'll call Linda, came from England. She said England had researched the subject of virginity on a wide scale. The study concluded that sexual incompatibility was rare. She said in those few cases where couples were sexually incompatible, couples normally worked things out. If they loved each other, they stayed together. Unfortunately, I could not obtain a copy of the study Linda mentioned. Linda also stated the research shows more problems exist with people having sex before marriage.

On a similar talk show, virgin men (older than teenagers) discussed celibacy. One man profoundly said: "I want to give my future wife the best gift I can possibly give her. And to me that is the gift of never comparing her to someone else." It was a lovely thing to say. This man was no wimp. He was the type of guy any of us would be proud to bring home.

In an article in the *Tulsa World* on Sunday, July 5, 1992, Curtis Austin of the *Dallas Morning News* states: "At least one national survey indicates that marriage may be more likely to fail if preceded by cohabitation."

The University of Wisconsin surveyed 13,017 Americans in 1987 and 1988 and discovered that "couples who had lived together before marrying were 40 percent more likely to be divorced within a decade than couples who did not." However, it goes on to say that living together may not be the whole story, but *the couples who would consider this type of living arrangement have "other traits" that might make them more likely to be candidates for divorce court.*

The article paraphrases Brenda Phillips, a visiting sociology professor at Southern Methodist University: "The same less-traditional view of marriage that allows couples to cohabit beforehand may also make them more likely to dissolve a troubled marriage."

At the lowest end of the scale, violent crimes against women have become rampant. Why? With all the sexual freedom, why so much anger?

Is it possible that when sex was saved until marriage, men expected to be rejected in their sexual advances? Now men expect to be accepted. Now only a few men might be constantly rejected. Would this make these men angry? Would they tend to hate women?

Being single is more difficult than being married. It is a painful state of living.

God's best is still for man and woman together.

Consequence No. 4 — Spiritual

Have you noticed? There are many couples in the church who are involved in sex outside of marriage. If you notice, those involved usually have other major spiritual problems.

One problem with the commission of this sin is it closes the "windows of heaven" — greatly hindering your flow of blessings from above. The closed windows may be due to the sin itself, but it is possible it is your disrupted relationship to God.

You have a hard time believing God will bless you while you are living in sin. You may not pray often. You may not attend church often. You feel convicted by the Holy Spirit of your misdeed. If you don't believe God will answer your prayers because of your sin, you probably won't ask for His help. Odds are you will remove yourself from fellowship with God. You might even decide being a Christian is too hard.

For example, with a history of drinking and driving, I would not expect my earthly father to buy me a new car. I would not consider asking him. It does not mean he would not buy me a car if I asked him. In the natural, I would have trouble believing Dad would do this for me. So I would not ask. I cut myself off from a possible blessing.

It is to my benefit to believe that those windows of heaven will be open. So, if I stay clear of sin, I have a tendency to believe I deserve to have my prayers answered.

Besides, why take a chance on closing the windows of heaven by involving yourself in a liaison that is not blessed by God? Then you do not need to worry about your blessings. They will come.

Being in a sinful relationship is spiritual suicide.

Does it make sense?

Chapter 7

Married Is Better!

As miserable as are many singles with the loneliness and boredom, I always wonder — why so many divorces? What do people expect to gain by divorcing?

Have you noticed how some married people appear jealous of your single status?

They see you do not answer to anyone, but they don't realize being alone also means usually no one cares.

They seem annoyed you do not cook dinner every night, but they do not know nightly you eat alone.

They seem envious you can read in bed all night long, but they forget that no one else shares your bed.

Yes, you can watch whatever you want on television, but TV may be your only entertainment for weeks.

Sadly, many married people covet the single lifestyle. They decide to divorce, only to discover, too late, that it was not the answer. They merely exchange one set of problems for another, and that is probably the best they can expect.

Being single is not glamorous. It is a lifestyle contrary to our God-given nature.

Even the most independent of my single friends would prefer to be in a good marital relationship. This is contrary to what they spout firmly to anyone who listens. When pressed, the truth comes out. Deep down these self-sufficient women want a loving relationship with *one* someone special. They do not want to relinquish certain parts of their freedom, but having a man around is important.

On a recent television talk show, three gorgeous career women in their thirties admitted they, indeed, made a mistake. They decided to establish their career first. Now they can find no one. The glory of their careers meant absolutely nothing when no one was there to share their glory.

Remember, the Bible tells us "The Lord God said, 'It is not good for the man to be alone. I will make a helper suitable for him' " (Gen. 2:18). Is that why God made two sexes?

When God made Adam and Eve, God blessed them. He said to them "Be fruitful and increase in number" (Gen. 1:28). So, God blessed man and woman with sex from the very beginning of our existence on the earth.

Again, I wonder if God did not have love and intimacy in mind when He created sex.

As an independent single, you would not wed just anybody. Still you probably would concede you do miss the loving companionship that should come from marriage. Even in the most despicable marriage you recall good times you can store away in your treasure chest of cherished memories. These memories incite yearnings for a perfect union.

Sadly, single women who want to marry actually sabotage their own interests by giving in to fornication. Men find fornication "fun." As one pastor recently stated, we should be careful not to indulge in fornication. We might find out how much fun it can be.

Of course, there is another truism, "Who will buy the cow when the milk is free?"

I do not believe most single women, especially Christian women, find sex outside of marriage "fun," long range. It might be enjoyable while in the process of indulging, but the next day, what about your conscience?

By allowing yourself the luxury of being seduced, you sanction the behavior and allow your man the benefit of not committing. Have you noticed that some men like the fun without all the responsibility? If your man wants you to shack up, odds are you are unequally yoked with a non-believer. Besides, guess who gets stuck with the responsibility if things do not go as planned?

Many women fear they will lack a mate more than they fear and reverence God. They decide they must "put out" or they will not find and keep a man. It became obvious to me, *if you "put out" you will get "left out" of God's best blessings.* Why take the chance?

Are you married, and reading this book because you are considering divorce? Is it possible you are giving up your marriage prematurely?

Based on my studies, many women, maybe even most women, who decide to leave the marriage, quickly realize the mistake. With this in mind, is there perhaps an interim step? Might you hammer out arrangements for temporary alternate living arrangements to salvage the marriage? I always told my husband I believed we would stay married forever if he lived elsewhere. This his pride would not allow.

Perhaps living single before the decision to divorce would preview the lifestyle. This arrangement might steer you away from the finality of divorce court.

Sadly, after a person gets dumped, normally they adamantly declare they will never hurt like that again. They protect themselves. They build walls. After the broken heart of a divorce, these walking wounded go on with their lives.

After divorce, "dumpees" loath the idea of returning to the same spouse and the same relationship for fear of getting dumped again. There is truly nothing like the pain of a divorce you did not want.

It will take a massive change in attitude for you and your spouse to put the marriage back together again. It can happen. With prayer, and sometimes separation for restoration, God can do it. But wouldn't it be so much easier if a divorce were not part of the picture? Wouldn't be easier if a separation were the first step?

One thing to remember, if God closes the door to a relationship, He simply has something better. I have learned to allow this thought to encourage me. Every time someone special does not work out, this thought keeps me going — He has something better. I cannot wait.

* * *

We are to praise the Lord no matter what happens, in every situation, for this is His will for us. "I will extol the Lord at all times; his praise will always be on my lips" (Ps. 34:1). "Give thanks in all circumstances, for this is God's will for you in Christ Jesus" (1 Thess. 5:18). We are to count everything in our life for joy. "Consider it pure joy, my brothers, whenever you face trials of many kinds, because you know that the testing of your faith develops perseverance" (James 1:2-3).

There was something I read recently on a DaySpring greeting card:

> We should fear only if
> The Lord were not in control. . . .
> We should worry only if
> The Lord were not able to meet our needs. . . .
> We should strive only if
> The Lord were not our Shepherd. . . .
> We should grieve only if
> The Lord were not risen![9]

* * *

What steps can you take as a single woman to protect yourself against the sinfulness surrounding you?

Can you learn to "count it all joy" when faced with diverse trials?

And, if it is God's best plan to have a husband, this question plagues single women everywhere: "If I do not put out, how can I find a spouse?"

Section Two: The Revelations

Chapter 8

A New Perspective on This Love Business

What exactly does the Bible say about sex?

Is it a basic need, like food and shelter?

When is it a sin?

And how on earth can you really avoid this temptation?

Do we control our sexual desires?

Is it too hard to remain holy?

And if I cannot control my sexual desires, is it really possible to live as a Christian? Should I try?

After feeling the spiritual release when I told Charles my decision, I decided to do some research. Although this study does not include everything I discovered, anyone struggling with temptation should find the information helpful.

The Bible warns us in 1 Corinthians 6:9-10:

> Do you not know that the wicked will not
> inherit the kingdom of God? Do not be deceived:

> Neither the sexually immoral nor idolaters nor
> adulterers nor male prostitutes nor homosexual
> offenders nor thieves nor the greedy nor drunk-
> ards nor slanderers nor swindlers will inherit the
> kingdom of God.

Incidentally, if you idolize the person you love, that is idolatry!

How many of the sins listed deal with sex? Why so many?
Does it have to do with the commandment to love one another?

Reading this list, I am reminded of a time I was consulting
in personnel for a local firm. Francis was head of the benefits
section for the company. Close to the same age, we spent some
time together and I thoroughly enjoyed her company. Fairly quiet
most of the time, I should have known by the natural red hair
that there was a fire in her tank.

One day Francis came in late, her brown eyes road mapped
with red and outlined with puffiness. When I asked her the problem, she brushed it off at first. Later, at lunch in a private room at
the plant, Francis told the catalyst for her mood. Her back straight-
ened, her voice steeled, and her tears gathered in pools ready to
spill at the slightest provocation. She was angry. She was confused, outraged, and at a loss to know what action to take.

"It's my repulsive brother-in-law," she said with barely
controlled fury. "That nauseating excuse for male flesh. . . ." She
paused to catch her breath. What was to come next had to be
hard for her to admit aloud. "He has been raping his own daughters. . . . How could he? He's evil. He's inhuman. I'd like to take
him out and publicly humiliate him, emasculate him, stake him
spread-eagled to the ground, sprinkle him with ants, and send a
video of his slow death to anyone else who even thinks of doing
this to their children."

Ouch! The described scene was reminiscent of some book
from years ago. To my way of thinking, the punishment was not
good enough for this creep.

My analytical mind started working. What was it about the
act that disgusted us so much?

Light bulbs! Immediately the answer came. The reason it

disgusted us? We knew what that act would do to the little girls for the rest of their life. We knew the pain. We knew the trauma. We knew that what this father did was not an act of love. No consideration was given in any way by the father to the feelings and future of his own precious daughters.

Okay, love being the lowest (or should I say highest) common denominator for a Christian, shall we look again at the list of things in 1 Corinthians 6:9-10? If we engage in any of these things, are we acting in a loving way toward others? What about the Ten Commandments? Are they not a list of things that teach us how to love one another? Before we had the Ten Commandments was there a standard of love?

Setting out on this quest to discover exactly what the Bible said, I discovered a point of view. If I put myself in the position of a parent, I gain perspective and my understanding increases. Over and over again God refers to himself as our Father and us as His children. And what greater love is there but the love of a parent for their child?

Why would a parent tell a child not to do something?

I would tell my child not to do something if it hurt her or if it made her unhappy. My purpose is not to spoil her fun. I want her to have fun. I want her to be happy. Odds are I know more about what makes her happy long-range than she does.

Could it to be? I wondered. Could it be that God gave us this list of sins for us to know what brings us unhappiness? Could it be He wants us to be happy?

I'm not talking of hedonistic happiness and its self-only reality. The happiness of which I speak is a contentment, a self-satisfaction, a self-respect. Your contentment comes from doing the right thing, the loving thing, the godly thing.

Ah, a new way to look at God! Not the temperamental God who loved us only if we were good enough. Not a God of conditional love. No, we are unconditionally loved, as is described in 1 Corinthians 13. Every sin we ever commit, past, present, and future, was nailed to the cross with Jesus. Through His blood, God sees us as righteous. We do this by believing in the One He sent. "Then they asked him, 'What must we do to do the works God requires?' Jesus answered, 'The work of God is this: to believe in the one he has sent' " (John 6:28-29).

What a deal! What's so hard about that?

Paul learned to be content in any situation, whether good times or bad, whether in prison or on the high seas.

Is that what God wants for us?

Certainly! Otherwise He would not be a God of love. Why would He put His Son through the Cross if not for His love of man?

Do you understand how much He loves you? Do you realize what He wants for you?

This book grew out of my concern for those who came to our church for counseling. People who loved God. They wanted to do their best to please Him. Yet somewhere, in some area of their life, they were not yet living in victory or contentment.

One woman in particular stormed into the church lobby one Sunday. "If I don't get some help," she said in a voice dripping with venomous anger, "I'll just walk out that door and end it all."

Coming in the door on my way to the phones to answer the prayer lines I just happened upon her tirade as it was taking place.

"I don't want to talk with you," she declared hysterically when I offered assistance. "I want to talk with a pastor."

An attractive lady, fiftyish, she sported a scar on her throat underneath a gold chain where her cross dangled. Her short-cropped grayish-blonde hair was fixed in a style more reminiscent of the fifties. She looked on the matronly-side, not the least bit the hysterical type.

Never had I faced such anger.

Finally, with another prayer counselor, we calmed her down and we were able to get her story.

The lady I'll call Rose told of tribulations and trials encompassing every area of her life. She lost a husband to divorce, she had suffered thyroid cancer, she lost her job, and she was having major problems with her daughter and son-in-law. She was on the brink of having more than she could handle.

Rose was mad. Her anger hit us like a fist. She could not get help. She did not know what to do.

Rose said her daughter was not allowing her to see her

grandbabies. According to Rose, her son-in-law was the culprit. She wanted him out of her life and her daughter's life. She wanted him gone.

Rose knew she was wrong to nurture this unforgiveness. She knew she was required to forgive him. She could not do it by herself. She wanted to. Her spirit was willing, but her flesh was weak.

"I know I'm going to hell, but. . . ." — if she said it once, she said it 12 times.

Another time during my weekly Bible fellowship group a classy lady joined us. Impeccably dressed in a designer jogging suit, her red hair shining in the warm light from the fireplace, Margie looked appropriate for a country club gathering. Margie is a close friend I have known for many years, and her disclosure surprised me greatly.

"My dad was a pastor," Margie shared. "He died early. In his forties." I relate this only to show how close to knowledge Margie was with a father who was a pastor . . . yet she was so far away from knowing the truth. She did not have personal knowledge. Not until years later.

"We lived in Independence, Kansas. My father preached a sermon in Wichita. On the way home from that service, the Lord spoke to him that he would be called home soon. He did not know why, but he just knew he was going." You could tell this affected Margie greatly. Her eyes swam with tears as she continued. "He wasn't even sick. Dad came home that night and told mom, 'Hon, now the Lord has told me I'm going home. I don't know how I'm going, but if I get sick or if I'm close to death, please do not pray for me. If you do I will live, and He does not want that right now.' Dad never understood why, but he died within that year at the age of 42. Perhaps the Lord needed a soldier in heaven. Who knows."

Needless to say, Margie and her family were devastated, but spiritually prepared. They had received the prophecy from their father. They did not pray for his survival.

You can see how Margie was raised. You can see her faith. The problem came later, when she felt confined, restricted, and unloved by her Heavenly Father.

You see, Margie believed legalistically. She believed in punishment . . . severe punishment.

"I believed that every time I did something wrong," Margie shared with tears streaming down her cheeks, "God would kick me out of heaven."

Both the incident with Rose and the incident with Margie occurred in the same week. When I heard this same theme, that they would be kicked out of heaven, that did it. I had to find a way to let people know.

God is not going to kick them out of heaven willy-nilly. God loves them.

Neither Margie nor Rose understood. When we learn how much God loves us, we have no fear. We do not worry about punishment. To paraphrase the Scripture, the man who fears does not understand God's love (1 John 4:18).

You are not to condemn yourself for any sin *unless* you are unwilling to repent.

"Egad," you probably are saying to yourself. "That means I have to stop sinning on my own. I don't think I can. And I won't be a hypocrite."

Okay, it's hard. But what is meant by the word repent?

The teaching I heard in the past on repentance is not what the Bible says. It is not deciding to turn from sin by your own will power. It is not *trying* to do it yourself. To repent means you decide to turn it over to God and rely on Him to work it out.

Both Rose and Margie, when they heard this, walked out of the church and the meeting knowing that their love for God and His love for them was sufficient. They walked away knowing that His faith was sufficient.

They walked away understanding that even their faith is not theirs. They cannot boast about it. Their faith has been authored and developed by someone else. "Let us fix our eyes on Jesus, the author and perfecter of our faith" (Heb. 12:2). Jesus is handling it for them. He is bringing them, step by step, to where He wants them to be. "If the Lord delights in a man's way, he makes his steps firm; though he stumble, he will not fall, for the Lord upholds him with his hand" (Ps. 37:23).

Once we learn this, we fully understand the Scripture about

perfect love casting out all fear. "There is no fear in love. But perfect love drives out fear, because fear has to do with punishment. The one who fears is not made perfect in love" (1 John 4:18). The perfect love comes from the Father to us. And He loves us, to use a psycho-babble word, unconditionally. God will not let things happen to those who are totally surrendered to Him, except those things that build character, patience, perseverance, and faith. No matter what happens to a child of God, in the end, God will use it for His glory. He will take a mess and make a glorious message.

* * *

What exactly is sin?
What did our forefathers mean by fornication?
What does the Bible say about sex after marriage?
Why would I want to remain celibate?

Chapter 9

Sin Has a Bad Rap

As a parent, what would I tell my child about sin?

First, there are things my daughter Stacey does that make me unhappy. I want her to follow my directions, even though it is not strictly for her good or her happiness.

For example, it disappoints me when she argues with me, when she wants to have the last word. I bet God feels the same way.

Also, it angers me when I tell Stacey not to borrow things without my permission, and she "borrows" them anyway. I say "borrow" lightly, because they often become missing pieces in an endless maze of friend's homes. I ask where a certain dress is, and it's at Kelly's or Tiffany's or Gretchen's. And the location changes each time I ask.

Almost a matter of stealing rather than borrowing, I feel violated and taken advantage of. Not just because of the objects, but also my goodwill.

This must be how God felt when He gave Adam and Eve just one commandment: Do not eat of this tree. They had access to every other tree in the Garden except the tree of the knowledge of good and evil. Only one tree were they to avoid.

In the same way, Stacey has access to every other thing in my house, except my personal things. When Adam and Eve defied God, it was like my daughter defying me about my clothes. I imagine God was furious with Adam and Eve because He was blatantly disregarded and disrespected.

I was furious with Stacey for the same reason. Knowing that I meant so little to Stacey that she would prefer to hurt me than to do without my things, I was terribly wounded.

The pain came from the knowledge of her apparent lack of love for me, not for the actual missing pieces. I know she loves me. Yet, I want her to learn she must consider the feelings of others. I want her to learn to show love not simply give it lip service.

Did Adam and Eve realize they were not showing God the respect He deserved?

Did they realize they were not showing Him love?

Did they appreciate Him for all the things He had done for them?

Did Adam and Eve realize how saddened God was by their actions?

Stacey acted against my will, as when we sin, we act against God's will.

It hurts me, makes me sad, and I do get mad when my daughter openly defies me. Even worse, I grieve when I see Stacey in pain or heartbroken or unhappy. Also, I am filled with much joy when Stacey is happy.

I would be horrified to know Stacey was miserable, especially if she had chosen it for herself. For example, if Stacey was on drugs or alcohol, I could not help her unless she wanted my help. She would have to ask. Stacey must make the choice to turn away from some things before my help would do her any good. Otherwise, she would do it again. If she did not see where she had gone wrong, then she would just repeat the error. If she did not see the benefit to avoid or the harm to continue, she would carry on, business as usual.

Should Stacey come to me for help, then she would recognize that she could not do it alone. She would recognize that she needed support. Her decision to accept my help, coupled with my ability to help, might be all she would need to extricate herself from her addiction. After all, I might be able to place her in a rehab, get her to AA or NA, or get her into a church group. As a loving parent, I would use everything I knew to help, once I knew she would accept it. Until then, I would be throwing away time, money, and effort with no results.

God is like any parent. It grieves Him when you are unhappy, and He is thrilled when you experience happiness and joy. I remember thinking, *So, that's what sin is. It's the warning system and instruction system of a loving parent.* I found confirmation in Psalm 19:7-11:

> God's laws are perfect. They protect us, make us wise, and give us joy and light. God's laws are pure, eternal, just. They are more desirable than gold. They are sweeter than honey dripping from a honeycomb. For they warn us away from harm and give success to those who obey them (TLB).

So, according to Psalm 19, here's what God's laws do:

1) They protect us.
2) They make us wise.
3) They give us joy and light.
4) They warn us away from harm.
5) They give success to those who obey them.

Isn't that just what you would do as a loving parent? Would you set rules and restrictions for these very same reasons? Would you want to protect your child from harm and unhappiness?

This same theme, that the commandments are for our own good, is repeated in Deuteronomy 10:12-13:

> And now, O Israel, what does the Lord your God ask of you but to fear the Lord your God, to walk in all His ways, to love Him, to serve the Lord your God with all your heart and with all your soul, and to observe the Lord's commands and decrees that I am giving you today *for your own good?* (italics added)

As a parent, I would tell my child, "Don't play with matches, you'll get burned." Our Heavenly Father does the same thing. He warns us what is right and what is wrong in His Word.

My child might get away with playing with a matches a few times. After all, the Bible tells us that sin is pleasant for a season. "He chose to be ill-treated along with the people of God rather than to enjoy the pleasures of sin for a short time" (Heb. 11:25). She might even get by many times before she gets burned. But sooner or later she will come running to me, crying because she burned her little finger.

I am sure God sits on His throne grumbling to himself in the same way any parent would in such an instance, "Oh, if only they would learn."

Chapter 10

If Sex Is a Sin, How Come It's So Much Fun?

Sex can be loads of fun and extremely pleasant for a season. But the consequences are among the most numerous and the most emotionally and physically ravaging it is possible to endure.

When facing consequences, as a Christian, you probably would come running to your Father, sorry you gave in to the pleasure of sin for a season. Perhaps Moses could teach us this lesson, for Hebrews 11:25 says about him: "Choosing rather to suffer affliction with the people of God than to enjoy the pleasures of sin for a season" (KJV).

Facing temptation, it is affliction to turn away from sex. But we have not even considered another possibility. What if you do give in, and this person wants to marry you, but you would not have them? Would it be a loving thing to do to lead him on?

Sex is the most intimate of human experiences. How, then, can you, as a Christian, be happy having an affair? No guarantees exist. It may not last until morning, much less a lifetime. And life-long intimacy is what we are all seeking. Unfortunately, engagements have ended at the altar.

Sure, marriages do end, too. Part of the reason is the lack of commitment we have come to expect. What are the odds that anyone will come into a marriage today without having multiple sex partners? What does that do to their commitment level?

Tim Stafford in his book *Sexual Chaos* says: "Intimacy is not love, exactly. It is a state that two people may feel for a night, for a month, or for a lifetime."[10]

Are you absolutely positive you will eventually marry? Would you be satisfied with knowing this time in bed with this man may very well be the last time in bed with this man? Can you handle knowing he will move on to someone else?

Would you willingly stake your salvation on him?

Not to say you would lose your salvation, but if you had to make a choice?

If you do break up after an affair, what then? Move on to another sexual partner? And the next time? And the next time? Are you willing to establish such a pattern?

Generally for women, when the body gets involved, the heart gets involved. The idea of commitment comes to mind. Unfortunately, this is not what many men think. They may be thinking only about relieving themselves sexually. If a man willingly jeopardizes his salvation on this issue, it is a good indication of his other convictions as a Christian.

When you do not involve sex, you can build a relationship first. You weed out sex hounds, interested only for physical relief. You discover who really loves you and who really loves the Lord. A man who truly loves God would not leave a woman who refuses sex before marriage. A man who truly loves God would not force you.

It has been my experience, and the experience of the single Christian women I know, that such men are extremely rare.

In fact, a humorous incident happened to illustrate how rare such men are. When I heard from the publisher that he wanted a few more case histories, I asked 400 people at my singles' Sunday school class for their input. Specifically, I asked for men to discuss what they expected in dating a Christian woman.

After the announcement, a friend came up to me. He shared that when I asked what men expect of a Christian woman, he heard someone behind him say, "Well, at least the missionary position."

This was in Sunday school. Need I say more?

You have to be so careful. You might find yourself emotionally attached to someone even without the sexual contact. After investing your emotional and spiritual self into someone, you might discover they are hiding a nature that goes against your belief system.

Watch out for men in sheep's clothing.

One friend, Scott, is on the mission's board of a local denominational church. I shared with him my views regarding sex, and he shared his with me. Scott tells me he would respect a woman's opinion. It would not stop him from seeing her if he really cared for her. Still he believes remaining celibate is "not practical," especially for men.

Scott believes celibacy is "not practical" for women as well as men. He tells me women call him occasionally to use him in ways he enjoys being used. I bet they are not truly Christian women. If they are Christian women, this lesson is yet to come to them. Meanwhile, Scott is like a stallion roaming the meadows of mares awaiting his attention.

Is this the type of conviction you want as a lifetime Christian partner?

Obviously, this man, as lovely and as caring as he is, has not made the Bible his source of wisdom and knowledge.

Gary, a single Christian minister, says, "It's the man's responsibility to not put the gal in that position." Gary says the sin of fornication is the first sign there is compromise in a man's life, that he has not put God first place, that his "love life" is not in the proper order.

Gary continues, "You (the woman) have a responsibility there also, that when he does fail, you don't." But sad to say, according to Gary, men have been "passing the buck since Adam." Adam allowed Eve to make a decision, followed her lead, then blamed her for the fall of man.

* * *

Once I realized God wants my joy and my happiness, I have known joy and happiness. "I have told you this so that my joy may be in you and that your joy may be complete" (John 15:11). After all, who would want to be a Christian if none of our prayers were answered. The best interest of the Kingdom is served when prayers are answered.

Once I realized that each time I sinned God was not about to kick me out of heaven, I have no more fear. In 1 John 4:17, it says, "In this way, love is made complete among us so that we will have confidence on the day of judgment, because in this world we are like him."

Once I knew I was loved, I knew He would make things right for me, as promised in Romans 8:28: "And we know that in all things God works for the good of those who love him, who have been called according to his purpose." I knew He would tell me what I was doing wrong for my own good.

Sin definitely has a bad rap.

Eventually, if you truly allow the Holy Spirit to lead you, *He* will not allow you to continue in sin. The Bible relates this in 1 John 5:18: "No one who has become part of God's family makes a practice of sinning, for Christ, God's Son, holds him securely and the devil cannot get his hands on him" (TLB).

According to this Scripture, if you listen to your conscience, the time comes when you not only *want* to turn from this sin, but you *will* turn from it.

Someone recently said, "Who are you to tell me these things?" It is not me . . . it is the Bible.

Is not one of the greatest areas of constant inquiry the area of, "How do we know God's will?" This is obviously the formula: "Do not conform any longer to the pattern of this world, but be transformed by the renewing of your mind. Then you will be able to test and approve what God's will is — his good, pleasing and perfect will" (Rom. 12:2):

1) Refuse to be conformed to the world;
2) Renew your mind in the Word;
3) Then you will be able to know God's will.

After you decide not to sin any longer and you give it to Jesus, do not condemn yourself if you fall periodically. The cleansing process sometimes takes several steps. Once you give it to Him with all your heart, all your mind, and all your body, then you can count on Him. He is the author of your faith, not you.

Would you expect your child to walk without falling the first time? Of course not! You would be crazy if you did not expect your child to fail. Eventually, you expect your child to learn to walk well enough not to fall, at least not often . . . but not at first. Why would God be any different?

If you fall, there is no reason to feel condemned. If you do feel condemnation, you are allowing Satan to accuse you. There is no condemnation in Christ Jesus. For Romans 8:1-2 says, "Therefore, there is now no condemnation for those who are in Christ Jesus, because through Christ Jesus the law of the Spirit of life set me free from the law of sin and death."

The moment you decide to do your best, the moment you repent in your spirit, your record is clean. If you asked God's forgiveness and asked for his help, you are totally and completely forgiven. God blots your sin off the books. God sees it no longer. Hebrews 10:17 says, "Then he adds: "Their sins and lawless acts I will remember no more." It does not exist.

In the world, if the law convicts you of a crime and later found you to be innocent, the government clears your public record. God pardons, too. Cast off any "imaginations" that you are not worthy (2 Cor. 10:5). God can take someone whose sins are as filthy as crimson and cleanse them as white as snow (Ps. 51:7).

King David is a man after God's own heart. The Hebrews knew David as beloved by God. Yet David violated one of the Ten Commandments, the sexual sin of adultery. This eventually resulted in the murder of his lover's husband.

Ultimately David repented and asked God's forgiveness.

What did God do? He allowed David to marry his lover.

David did suffer. Just read the Book of Psalms and you will see how much he suffered. David endured the consequences for his actions, but God did forgive him. God did not send the consequences, but he allowed them. David himself said he had never seen the Lord forsake a man who loves Him.

"I was young and now I am old, yet I have never seen the righteous forsaken or their children begging bread" (Ps. 37:25).

David included himself in this statement. Even though he violated two of the Ten Commandments, murder and adultery, God did not forsake him. God honors commitments made to Him, even if we forget to honor the commitments ourselves. He will bring you to a place of remembrance. If He must allow things to happen in your life before you turn to Him again, He will allow things to happen.

"I used to resent those bad times," Angela told me. Angela had been through some really hard times in her life, having been married twice, once divorced and once widowed. "I was mad at God for allowing them to happen. What had I done that was so bad?

"But you know, after a few bad times, I finally discovered that I tended to slip away from God when times were good. I guess that's normal, but it was during the bad times that I grew closer to God. It taught me a valuable lesson. Now I stay in close contact all the time."

You probably won't enjoy suffering the consequences of your own actions, as the writer of Hebrews 12:10-11 exclaimed: "Our fathers disciplined us for a little while as they thought best; but God disciplines us for our good, that we may share in his holiness. No discipline seems pleasant at the time, but painful. Later on, however, it produces a harvest of righteousness and peace for those who have been trained by it."

So does it not make logical sense abide with God?

* * *

Regarding sexual sin, 1 Corinthians 6:13-20 tells us specifically:

> But sexual sin is *never right*: our bodies
> were not made for that, but for the Lord and the
> Lord wants to fill our bodies with Himself. And
> God is going to raise our bodies from the dead
> by His power just as He raised up the Lord Jesus

Christ. Don't you realize that your bodies are actually parts and members of Christ? So, should I take Christ and join Him to a prostitute? *Never! And don't you know that if a man joins himself to a prostitute, she becomes part of him and he becomes a part of her?* For God tells us in the Scripture that *in His sight* the two become one person. But if you give yourself to the Lord, you and Christ are joined together as one person. That is why I say run from sex sin. No other sin affects the body as this one does. When you sin this sin it is against your own body. Haven't you learned that your body is the home of the Holy Spirit God gave you, and that He lives within you? For God has bought you with a great price. So, use every part of your body to give glory back to God, because He owns it (TLB, emphasis added).

In the midst of my affair with Charles I tried my best to rationalize what I was doing. I searched the Bible. I found instances where men had many wives and many concubines. That did not strike me as particularly fair.

If sex is so much fun, how come it is a sin?

I noticed Abraham, Sarah, and Hagar. After years of waiting for God's promise, Sarah remained barren. She became discouraged and gave Abraham her maidservant, Hagar. This gesture apparently was not unusual or unnatural for that time in history.

Nowhere in the Bible did it say specifically that sex outside of marriage was a sin. At least not in those exact words. Nor did I find where fornication was explicitly defined as "sex outside of marriage."

I wanted to know what the original writers meant by fornication or sexual immorality. Did they mean sex was a sin when two people love each other, but simply chose not to marry?

In the Hebrew/Greek dictionary I looked up the word fornication. It was defined "*illicit* sex." What did that mean? In Biblical times Roman orgies, sex with animals, and other forms of deviant sexual practices were common. Could that be what the writers meant by fornication — deviant sex?

What was "illicit" sex? According to my dictionary, "illicit" simply means unlawful or illegal. I could not find anywhere, even in Leviticus or Deuteronomy, anything mentioning the legality of sex outside of marriage. And how legal were King Solomon's 300 concubines, mentioned in 1 Kings 11:3?

The Scriptures warn in Proverbs against the temptation of a prostitute. With this in mind, I used the Scripture from 1 Corinthians 6 to justify my behavior. After all, I am not a prostitute.

I continued to justify my action.

At Bible study I told everyone about my investigation. The group leader said something profound. "Donna," he said, "I am not going to argue with you about this. I am going to pray that God will convict you."

He did and God did.

God continued to deal with me in my spirit, my conscience. Eventually I could no longer stand the pressure and the weight of the burden of this sin. I simply could no longer stand "my spirit (being) heavy within me" (Ps. 69:20). I decided it was more important to please God than to please myself.

Gary, a single church counselor, says, "Why not be single and have God's best? It is certainly better than compromising and voiding God's blessings."

That's when I realized how it's done. I needed to put on "the garment of praise for the spirit of heaviness" (Isa. 61:3).

What happened after I decided to repent of the sin of fornication?

I saw Charles again. I faced almost overwhelming temptation again. I allowed him to hold me and kiss me again. All the while, my inner voice was rooting me on. "Tell him no," it said. "Go on, Donna, do it . . . tell him no." It hounded me and hounded me until, thank God, I finally said a feeble "No." The second time I said "No" it was with a great deal more enthusiasm.

When this happened, all the oppression, the heaviness of my spirit, lifted. It's such a cliché, but so true, I felt as though a ton of bricks lifted from me. Finally, after two years of oppression and depression and every other "ession," I once again experienced peace of mind.

I believe God orchestrated Charles coming back into my life. I believe He did it so I could make the choice to follow my conscience. To follow Him.

God wanted me to stop my idolatry, and idolize Him, not man. God wanted me to be happy.

Although sex is momentary fun, more to be desired is the prolonged joy God wants for me.

Yes, sin certainly does have a bad rap.

Chapter 11

Step #1 –
Why Not Take
All of Me!

You must totally surrender your will to God.

Total surrender! That's what He wants. And willingness to surrender begins with understanding God loves you. He gave His best for you. He loved you as a sinner. He does not love you less as His child.

The story of Louise is a good illustration of how total surrender can work in your life.

* * *

Sitting side by side answering the prayer line at church one Friday night, Louise and I were sharing the week's events. After telling her about my book and hearing her tale, we both realized her account was anointed to be told. Having never divulged the incident to anyone before, she knew why she faced the situation. Louise said she was revealing it now because she wanted others to know of God's amazing protection and power to rescue His surrendered children.

Louise, a born-again Christian for years, did not marry a believer the first time around. She found herself divorced and backslidden. She was mad at God. Why had He allowed this to happen?

After her husband left, Louise met another man. A dramatic and elegant black woman, she immediately attracted Dale's attention. Dale is an alluring hunk of a man who just happened to be white and blond and wealthy.

Dale treated Louise like a lovestruck schoolboy treats his first love, catering to her in ways her husband never did. And it follows that Louise fell for the big guy in a mighty big way.

I cannot recall the circumstances of their break up, but they did break up.

After recommitting her life to the Lord, Louise moved away from her hometown in New Jersey, away from Dale, and began attending a Bible institute in Tulsa.

More than two years passed when Louise received an invitation to a wedding in her hometown. She was thrilled. She flew off with great anticipation of seeing all her friends again, and possibly seeing Dale for old times' sake. Perhaps he, too, had changed.

The wedding was a marvelous success, and sure enough, Dale attended. Champagne flowed from gold-toned fountains at the reception, and Louise found her crystal goblet constantly brimming with the bubbly.

The next thing Louise remembers of that night is climbing into a hot tub with Dale. She remembers Dale looking up at her as she, clothed in nothing but a smile, stepped into the churning water. She says she will always remember his words, though she recalls very little else of that night. Dale said: "Louise, I know how much your faith means to you and I know how much you will regret this in the morning. I will not lay a hand on you. . . ."

Louise rejoices that even in this situation when she was more than willing, God was with her. As the Bible tells us, no temptation comes our way except what is common. But, good news — God will not allow us to be tempted beyond what we can bear. And when we are tempted, we are assured that He will provide a way of escape.

"No temptation has seized you except what is common to man. And God is faithful; he will not let you be tempted beyond what you can bear. But when you are tempted, he will also provide a way out so that you can stand up under it" (1 Cor. 10:13).

Louise knows she experienced God's protection in this tempting situation for one reason — she had sincerely committed her way to the Lord.

Sure, Louise may have missed the mark by over-indulging in alcohol. The liquor did diminish her resistance to temptation. She may have missed the mark in lusting after Dale, but God knew her heart.

God allowed Dale, even though not a practicing Christian, to see this momentary act of lust would later cause Louise tremendous heartache. He was acting in God's love. God worked in and through Dale to provide Louise with a way of escape.

Louise returned to Tulsa with a clear conscience and in awe of God's rescuing power. Little did she know that some months later her story would be used as a message to others.

Louise left Dale that weekend knowing he would always have a place in her heart because of his unselfish act of sacrifice. She knows she probably will never see him again and it is okay with her.

It is God's plan Louise wants.

It is His best that gives her joy.

To Know Him Is To Love Him

One thing worries me, without which everything else in this book will be about as useful as handles on a wheel. Using the handles, you might think you're accomplishing something, but . . . take the handles off, let the wheel roll, and you really get somewhere. That thing? Relying on your own intelligence is using handles, for we read in Proverbs 3:5-6: "Trust in the Lord with all your heart and lean not on your own understanding; in all your ways acknowledge him, and he will make your paths straight." Knowing Him is letting the wheel roll.

I am concerned about those thousands and thousands of "Christians" who really aren't Christian at all.

Even if you know absolutely for certain that you are a Christian, bear with me on this, please. I plead with you for all those who need this information as once I did. You could be instrumental in making a difference in someone's life. And, after all, is that not our purpose?

As for me, I professed for years to be a Christian. If anyone had asked me, I would have argued with them profusely. But I was not.

In my previous life, I might have picked up this book as a "Christian." I might have read the book cover to cover, and had this portion been left out, I would not have been able to assimilate this information into my daily life. Frankly, I do not want to waste effort, either yours, mine, or a publisher's by allowing that to happen. My prayer is that you take this information and live the joyful life God wants for you.

How do you know you are a Christian?

There is a test. Ask yourself these questions from 2 Corinthians 13:5: "Check up on yourselves. Are you really Christians? Do you pass the test? Do you feel Christ's presence and power more and more within you? Or are you just pretending to be Christians when actually you aren't at all?" (TLB).

When I was a "professing Christian" I did not feel Christ's presence. I did not know His power. I thought He was someone I went to only when I had problems. Never did it occur to me (until I read Colossians 2:6) that I could go to Him every moment of every day for every concern in my life. Never did I realize how much I could turn my cares over to His care.

"Cast all your anxiety on him because he cares for you" (1 Peter 5:7).

Where do you stand? In my opinion, at least five categories of people exist based on how they relate to the gospel. Into which category do you place yourself?

The Unbeliever — If this is you, you remain unconvinced about God. Certainly you don't believe in Jesus. The Bible? Who wrote it? Just men!

Will you ridicule when you read this information?

Charlene did. She thought it was hogwash. Charlene is a tall, blonde attorney. She relied on her intelligence as well as her looks to get ahead in life. So far, she succeeded fairly well, but felt something missing.

"But you know," she told me later, "much of what you wrote is God's Word. Although my heart was almost totally numb, the Word did have an effect. A small inner voice kept working on me. I visualized in my mind's eye an angel on one shoulder and a devil on the other."

If only Satan were a cute character, we would understand how insignificant he is to the believer. Unfortunately, he is the great deceiver. Ask him a question, and he will tell you a lie — always.

"I kept hearing that inner voice," Charlene continued. "I was skeptical, but deep in my spirit I kept hearing the question, 'What if it is true?' I wondered. So, I decided to simply believe."

What is believing? It is accepting information, deciding to trust it is truth. Believing is a decision. It is an act of the will, something you do, just like Charlene did when she decided to believe. Remember the Missouri saying, "I have to see it to believe it"? With the Christian faith, the opposite is true. "You have to believe it before you will see it."

The Alleged Christian — A friend, Jessie, recently related to me, "This was my level of belief for 28 years," she said as she wiped a happy tear from her cheek. "I claimed I was a Christian. I thought I was a Christian. But I did not believe Jesus was the Son of God. Jesus was just a man who walked this earth, just like Buddha or Mohammed. I wanted to believe, but I was skeptical. Some Christian."

Jessie said she had no idea Jesus could come into her life and help her with decisions. Even after she asked Him to live in her, she remained skeptical.

"I wanted signs," Jessie said. "I did not see any at first. I did not know how to let go and let God. I did not know how to 'leave the driving' to Him."

Is this how you feel?

You probably realize if you refuse to open your heart to

Jesus, there is a possibility of eternal consequences. If you do open your heart and allow Jesus to come in, what consequences then?

"Now, I cannot think of any," Jessie replied in response to this question. "But B.C., Before Christ, I could think of a thousand and more excuses."

Why don't people allow Jesus into their hearts?

The most common response? They did not want to give up their fun.

To some, sins represent fun. Thus the reason for the book. To show you have more fun, more joy, more happiness with Jesus than you ever did without Him.

One of the funniest reasons for not accepting Jesus came from one of my best friends. She did not want to preach to pygmies in the African jungles. That was more than ten years ago. She has since become a born-again Christian, and Jesus has not sent her to Africa once.

I caution you, after you accept that God did send His Son to earth in human form, it may not be enough. After you accept Jesus did die for your sins, you may have only allowed Him to be your Saviour. Jesus wants to be your Lord.

The Saved Christian — If this is you, you know who Jesus is. You have accepted the salvation He offers. You have your fire insurance to avoid the lake of fire, but you have not given Him control. He wants to become your savior *AND* your lord. You have not yet made Him Lord.

I know you know people like this.

"I don't have to worry about this," said Eric, when asked about his numerous affairs. "I've been saved. Once saved, always saved."

Really? Maybe so, but how about God's best? How about His blessings? How about God answering prayers?

Saul ran into this problem (1 Sam. 13 and 14). He had an appointment to meet with Samuel on a certain day. When Samuel did not appear that day and Saul's people were leaving him, Saul got scared. He did something totally against God's commandments. He, though not a priest, made an offering to the Lord. During the time of the Mosaic covenant, people were judged by the law. They were not yet free of the law — Jesus had not yet died on the cross.

Later, Saul went into battle against the Philistines. But he did something without first checking with God. He used fear tactics to motivate his people. Not a loving thing to do. Saul required his people to take an oath that any man who ate any food before evening would be cursed. So, none of the men tasted any food during the heat of battle and they were weak and faint and did not rejoice in their victory.

Finally, by evening when the oath expired, starved men devoured their spoil, not bothering to cook it. They ate raw meat with blood — also totally against God's laws.

What happened later when Saul asked for a counsel with God? Simple. He did not get an answer. Saul had blocked his blessings by his disobedience.

Do you want your blessings blocked?

Are you simply allowing Jesus to be a Saviour?

The Unbelieving Believer — Jane was an Unbelieving Believer before she came to me. Jane is a realtor who attends church almost every time the door is open. Jane's blazing brown eyes mirrored her bursting curiosity.

"Jesus was my Lord," she reported. "I would seek Him first when making decisions. I would strive to allow Him to lead me in every area of my life. I even learned to walk by the promptings of the Holy Spirit. But I was still missing something. I did not believe the Bible is God revealed on the earth. I did not believe the Bible is truth. Oh, bits and pieces you believe, but not all.

"I had not read the Bible through and I made judgments on the contents based on what I heard from others."

Is this not what many of us do? I'm sure all of the people Jim Jones duped would have dealt with his death drink differently had they had a personal wealth of knowledge of Scripture.

"Don't get me wrong," Jane continued, "I did attempt to read the Bible, but I could not understand it. I noticed the promises in the Bible, but I did not believe they were for me."

Do you?

The Complete Christian — You believe everything the Holy

Spirit, Jesus, and the Lord God Almighty have ever revealed. You believe the Bible is God revealed on earth. You check everything you hear to be sure it lines up with the Scripture (Acts 17:11). You learn to flow in the gifts of the Spirit. The fruits of your labor are visible for all to see.

God willing, this is you.

If this is you, you have been blessed by God. He has chosen you to be among His children, those adopted into His family.

Decide to believe today, and you will be a complete Christian today.

* * *

Contemplating these categories, the Lord revealed a Scripture: "The time has come for judging the dead, and for rewarding your servants, the prophets and your saints and those who reverence your name" (Rev. 11:18;NIV).

You will note three categories of people rewarded in heaven:

1) *The Prophets* — possibly the complete Christians.

2) *The Saints* — I believe correspond to the saved Christians and the unbelieving believer. These people have a solid belief system, only they believe just a portion of the gospel.

3) *Those who reverence His name* — who believe on the name of Jesus Christ, our Lord. This group possibly falls into the saved Christian and possibly the alleged Christian. I don't know with certainty, but Jesus does. They stand a chance of "perishing" for lack of knowledge. "My people are destroyed from lack of knowledge. 'Because you have rejected knowledge, I also reject you as my priests; because you have ignored the law of your God, I also will ignore your children' " (Hos. 4:6).

Let me challenge you as someone once challenged me. If you are an unbeliever or you know someone who is, this information can mean the difference between eternal life or eternal death.

The Challenge

If I am wrong, Jesus is not alive and seated
at the right hand of God the Father in heaven.

If I am wrong, there is no heaven or hell.

If I am wrong, the Bible is not true.

If I am wrong, I lose nothing by believing what I believe and neither has the non-believer.

If, however, I am right, there is a Jesus who is alive and seated at the right hand of God the Father.

If I am right, there is a heaven and a hell.

If I am right, the Bible is true.

If I am right, I obviously lose nothing by believing what I believe. But the unbeliever loses eternity.

In either case, it makes logical sense I lose nothing by believing.

Even though it may appear to the unbeliever there is a 50-50 chance — not true. What's at stake is eternity. The stakes are maximum, the house limit. This is eternity, not just a card game or a roll of the dice for a billion dollar fortune. You can rebuild a fortune. The unbeliever will not be able to rebuild their eternity if I am right. When the hearse backs up to the door, there is no second chance. Life is not a dress rehearsal.

Are you willing to stake your everlasting future on your decision to reject this information?

Are you willing to allow your loved one to live without hearing the truth?

* * *

A surrendered life is the beginning of understanding and wisdom. You begin to have spiritual insight. You begin to understand how the woman of the world, which you once were, is baffled and bothered by your new found faith. First Corinthians 2:15-16 says, "The spiritual man makes judgments about all things, but he himself is not subject to any man's judgment: 'For who has known the mind of the Lord that he may instruct him?' But we have the mind of Christ." Your friends argue with you. They try to confound you. They pick apart parts of the Bible or your faith. They label you as a prude. They ask you questions meant to make a mockery of your belief system.

Rejoice! As a Christian, you actually do have within you a portion of the very thoughts and mind of Christ.

Stand firm when you face ridicule because of your stance on extramarital sex. You must be willing to seem a fool for His sake before you understand what joy it brings you. And when you do set aside the world's wisdom, which is foolishness to God, you will be on firmer ground. Continue to rely on your own brilliance, and God allows you to trap yourself, allows you to suffer the consequences.

"Do not deceive yourselves. If any one of you thinks he is wise by the standards of this age, he should become a 'fool' so that he may become wise. For the wisdom of this world is foolishness in God's sight. As it is written: 'He catches the wise in their craftiness' " (1 Cor. 3:18-19).

Okay, now you know to receive His help you must surrender everything. You surrender your cares and concerns. You surrender your thought life. You surrender your actions. You surrender your will power or lack of it, your ability to do things alone. For purposes of this book, most of all you surrender your sex life. Everything!

If you do not allow Jesus the right to be Lord to you, you are like a rebellious child. A child who does not understand it is for your own good when your father orders you not to play in the middle of the highway. You play there anyway. When semis fly around you, run you down, and accidents occur because of you, you learn why your father warned you to stay out of the street. Hopefully, you learn to be the child who sits in a porch swing watching peacefully the steady progress of eighteen wheelers past your house — a much better position to be in. Wouldn't you be much happier you decided to listen?

Don't you want Jesus to help you with everything?

Edward told me about a seminar at his church. Edward is an attractive, successful business man who once studied for and became an ordained minister. Eventually he became a divorce statistic and is still seeking the right woman.

"A psychologist was speaking," he related. "This is a respected doctor recognized in the community as a Christian. He said something that literally shocked me. He said we should not 'bother God with the little things in our lives like who to marry.'

"After I put my teeth back in my mouth, I argued with him, as I am prone to do. Isaac bothered God with this issue. His servant bothered with it. This issue is important to God, so it should be to us."

Jesus is Lord over your life anyway. Just because you don't agree with a particular president, using President Clinton as a good example, this doesn't mean he isn't the president. You might as well get used to the idea that the president of the United States is there and he is going to make policy decisions as long as he is there, policy decisions that affect your life.

If you choose to deny Christ's power in your life, you will not have His protection. You allow Satan a foothold by your unbelief, which we are commanded not to do (Eph. 4:27).

Did you know that Satan asks for permission to bother you? At least he asked permission to sift Peter like wheat. "Simon, Simon, Satan has asked to sift you as wheat. But I have prayed for you, Simon, that your faith may not fail. And when you have turned back, strengthen your brothers" (Luke 22:31-32;NIV).

He also asked permission to bother Job. " 'But stretch out your hand and strike everything he has, and he will surely curse you to your face.' The Lord said to Satan, 'Very well, then, everything he has is in your hands, but on the man himself do not lay a finger.' Then Satan went out from the presence of the Lord" (Job 1:11-12;NIV)

Put yourself in God's place just for a moment. Even as finite as you are and as infinite as He is, it's still possible to have some understanding. If your child did not listen, was rebellious, and you could do nothing, what would you do? Would you consider jailing him overnight? It might teach him a lesson. Would you consider kicking him out of your house, out of fellowship with you, until he straightens up? Sure you would.

Programs now exist to help the rebellious child get scared straight through tough love.

If your child did everything in his power, the best he could do to follow your guidelines, would you ever dream of going to such drastic measures?

If you knew that your child was going to cause another

person great heartache and financial destruction, would you want your child to be that uncaring? Would you do something to get her to sit up and take notice? Would you punish her in some way? If you could not get her attention, would you allow her to suffer the consequences of her actions?

* * *

Still skeptical? Remember, the unbelieving will also be in the lake of fire. "But the cowardly, the unbelieving, the vile, the murderers, the sexually immoral, those who practice magic arts, the idolaters and all liars — their place will be in the fiery lake of burning sulfur. This is the second death" (Rev. 21:8).

So simply choosing not to believe, and it is a choice, is choosing your own destruction.

If you are like I was and you cannot rationalize Jesus, then ask yourself these three questions:

1) If there is a God, could He not do anything He wanted to do?

2) If He wanted to send His Son in the form of a man, what would stop Him?

3) Would you want to know such a God and His Son?

If still skeptical, are you willing to be open? Then pray this prayer:

Lord Jesus, if You really do exist, if You really are the Son of God, I want to know You. If You are the Son of God, please come into my heart and live Your life through me. Be Lord of my life. If there is sin in my life, show me. Search my heart. Please forgive my sins and cleanse me from unrighteousness.

Are you now a new babe in Christ? One note of caution. Do not expect everything to happen immediately. For me, it did not. In fact, I fell away from church for several years before I was able to get some decent discipleship.

The most important thing you can do for yourself is to get into the Word of God. If you give it a chance, stick with it, and open your mind to its truth, you will soon agree this is the best investment you could ever make. Reading the Bible is like bowling or golf or bridge — you will never have it totally mastered.

Do these things, and expedite your blessings. Do not wait until you are in the middle of the highway with semis flying around you before you call on your Father. You want your blessings on the fast track, do you not?

* * *

Now if you are concerned about your sex life, what would you do?

If your answer is "Surrender all to God," you win!

Chapter 12

Step #2 — I Did It My Way?

Choose to Handle Your Sex Life God's Way.

Every time I hear alcoholism described as a disease, I get angry. It may become a disease, but in the beginning it is a decision to do it "their way." Everything we do in life starts with a thought or a decision.

Remember that first drink? If you have had the experience, you remember how nasty it tasted. The alcoholic had to choose to ignore the taste to continue with a second drink. Later, many have had to choose between their families and their bottle. Many have chosen their bottle. They cannot see themselves without their flask, but they can easily do without their family.

What angers me is that this attitude of disease takes the responsibility out of the individual's hands and places a medical excuse on a moral decision. Obviously, the easier thing to do is to never start something than to stop something you have started.

The same is true with sex. To lose your virginity in the first place, except in the case of rape, you probably made a decision to do so. To continue to have sex outside of marriage is continuing to make decisions.

Good Guilt

What about your conscience? Have you have become numb to that quiet small voice within? When you commit the sin of fornication that voice speaks. It says, "This is wrong. Don't do it!" If you continue to violate your own conscience, you are miserable. You feel lousy about yourself. Or you become defiant, demanding to know why God would give us sex, which is such a blessing, only to take it away. To you, it does not make sense, so you defy what your conscience tells you.

You may try rationalizing. You tell yourself everyone else is doing it. You tell yourself this sin is no worse than any other sin. Yet deep in your conscience you cannot hide from the guilt.

Guilt, unlike some teaching from modern secular counselors and motivational speakers, is not a useless emotion. Guilt is good and useful if applied appropriately. Guilt brings you to the point of decision. Why? Paul tells us in 2 Corinthians 7:10: "Godly sorrow brings repentance that leads to salvation *and leaves no regret*, but worldly sorrow brings death" (NIV, emphasis added).

And, God has written His law in your heart. We all know the Scripture that says we will know the truth and the truth will set us free (John 8:32, 36), but do we know the Scripture that leads into this? John 8:31 tells us how to know the truth: "If you continue in my Word, then are you my disciples indeed: And you shall know the truth and the truth shall make you free" (NIV).

In her song, "Tell Me What Love Is, Jesus," Nancy Honeytree relates just such a story:

It's an old familiar story
She was flattered, charmed, confused.
And they say it can't be wrong when it feels so right
But in the light of morning
All she felt was used
And she wishes now she'd never spent the night. . . .

It's an old familiar story
He just had to get involved,
Cause whatever feels so right just can't be wrong.
But when the light of morning
Brought more problems than it solved
And the feelings fade that once had seemed so strong.
Everybody knows the story
But this one ended differently,
Cause he and she both got down on their knees.
Praying please forgive me, Jesus.
Help me walk your way,
Cause I never want to break your heart like I did yester-
day.
Tell me what love is, Jesus.
I'd really like to know.
I'm beginning to doubt all the things I learned from the
TV and the radio.
Tell me what love is, Jesus.
How does it actually feel?[11]

Are our feelings not quite so important when love is real?

This is what Jesus does for you. You decide, surrender, and let Him work in your life, and *He* helps you walk His way. *He* cleanses you. *He* brings you from glory to glory. To progress from glory to glory, or from mountaintop to mountaintop, you must pass through valleys.

Like the couple in Nancy's song, your part is turn to Jesus and ask His forgiveness. Your part is to decide to do the best you can to avoid the sin in your life. In other words, your part is to decide to *be willing to be made willing* to follow Jesus. When you do, you soon realize how *God will help you follow through*. If you fail, just pick yourself up as any falling baby would, and try again. And again. And again. Soon, you walk without falling.

Not a pleasant thought or an easy task to let go of the man in your life. If you are living with him, letting go is especially difficult. Like many others, you may have lived this way so long you cannot see yourself living any other way. All your friends feel the way you once did because people generally cultivate friends who live like they do. You have no experience with those who try to live a life dedicated to pleasing God.

You have not yet realized that pleasing God pleases you.

What is hard to get across if you are living in this sin is it really is easy to make a change. When faced with the decision, leaving the situation appears overwhelming. *YOU* must take the step — no one else can do it for you. You must purpose in your heart that you are willing. Then be honest with your Father, God, that you cannot do it alone. Be honest. God knows you do not believe you have the power to do what needs to done. It won't be by your might. It won't be by your power. It can only happen by the power of His Spirit. "So he said to me, 'This is the word of the Lord to Zerubbabel: "Not by might nor by power, but by my Spirit," says the Lord Almighty' " (Zech. 4:6). Be honest. You need His help.

The Bible says in 1 John 1:9, "If we confess our sins, He is faithful and just to forgive us our sins, and to cleanse us from all unrighteousness" (KJV).

Turn the above Scripture around slightly and you see how He works. He will "cleanse you from all unrighteousness and forgive you . . . if you confess your sins." This does not say "if you have the will power to change." This does not say "if you stop sinning." All that is required is the confession of our sins. God knows that with the confession as a Christian, we want to do what's right.

Our conscience is one of many ways we are cleansed from unrighteousness. Remember, too, if you know what is right to do and then you do not do it, it is sin. This is touched on in James 4:17: "Anyone, then, who knows the good he ought to do and doesn't do it, sins."

What about that person who does *not* know what is right and sins, is it sin to him? Jesus says unless He teaches them, they would be blameless, they would not be guilty. "If I had not come and spoken to them, they would not be guilty of sin. Now, however, they have no excuse for their sin" (John 15:22).

This Scripture puts most who read this book in a dangerous position. You have been taught. You are now responsible.

We are warned yet again in Romans 14:23 (TLB): "But

anyone who believes that something he wants to do is wrong shouldn't do it. He sins if he does, for he thinks it is wrong, and so for him, it is wrong. Anything that is done apart from what he feels is right is sin" (TLB).

So, if you doubt or have an uneasy conscience about something you want to do, and then do it anyway, you are committing a sin. You are not true to your convictions and you do not act in faith. Anything that does not originate and proceed from faith is sin.

Again, God wants his children happy and joy filled. Obviously, if you are doing something you believe is wrong and an affront to God, it will have the opposite effect. Are you doing something without God's approval? As a Christian your spirit is in turmoil. The Holy Spirit will pester until you do something about it. Eventually you do not continue in sin. "What shall we say, then? Shall we go on sinning, so that grace may increase? By no means! We died to sin; how can we live in it any longer?" (Rom. 6:1-2).

Test yourself. The next time you tell a little white lie, how do you feel? Do you feel remorse immediately? Do you immediately ask forgiveness? Or each time the feeling arises, do you justify your behavior? Do you stuff?

We should be like Paul and strive always to keep our conscience clear. "So I strive always to keep my conscience clear before God and man" (Acts 24:16).

Just this morning I said a word in anger that I would normally never say. Immediately my spirit screamed at me. I repented of the anger, but I stewed most of the morning. How could I still do these things after walking with God this long?

Our conscience is a good gift God has given to mankind. Guilt is good.

Jesus prayed to the Father, "I do not pray that You should take them out of the world, but that You should keep them from the evil one" (John 17:15).

Here are four ways you can stand against evil and keep it out of your life:

1) *Submit to God, and resist the devil.* "Submit yourselves therefore to God. Resist the devil and he will flee from you" (James

4:7). Make Jesus Christ the Lord of your life, and come under His authority.

2) *Speak the Word aloud*. The promises of God contained in His Word, if believed and spoken aloud, will enable you to escape the evil that is in the world. "Whereby are given unto us exceeding great and precious promises: that by these ye might be partakers of the divine nature, having escaped the corruption that is in the world *through lust*" (2 Pet. 1:4). Jesus gave us an example of resisting and overcoming the devil with, "It is written," and the speaking of the appropriate Scripture promise for the particular situation. You raise up a standard against evil by speaking the Word aloud!

3) *Put on the whole armor of God* (Eph. 6:10-11). To put on the whole armor of God will enable you to stand against the wicked plots and schemes of the devil. The armor includes the breastplate of righteousness; girding your loins with truth; the preparation of the Gospel of peace for your feet; the helmet of salvation; the shield of faith with which to quench *every* fiery dart of the wicked; and the sword of the Spirit, which is the Word of God spoken aloud from your lips; and praying with all manner of prayer and supplication in the Spirit.

4) *"Keep yourself" under the Almighty's wings in fellowship, in speaking God's Word with authority, in prayer, praise and worship and in joy.* "We know that whosoever is born of God sinneth not; but he that is begotten of God keepeth himself, and that wicked one toucheth him not" (John 5:18).

It's time for you to rise up on the INSIDE, and not allow evil to run over your life anymore in the name of Jesus Christ of Nazareth.[12]

Chapter 13

Step #3 — Spirit Led

Allow yourself to be led by the Holy Spirit.

Do you want to know God's will for you?

Do you know what you must do to know God's will?

You know you must stay in communication with God to know His will.

For example, if you have good friends, you know them quite well. You speak with them each day, and you share your feelings and your cares and your concerns. You love each other. You know you would do anything for that friend and that friend would do anything for you.

What would happen, though, if, for no reason, your friend did not call for a week. Would you be hurt? Say she didn't call for a year, would she know how you were feeling? Would you have any idea what she was feeling?

Sure, it is possible for you to know that person well enough to know their character and general feelings, but you don't have a clue what's happened each day. You don't have a clue if she wants you or needs you for anything. You have no contact. You have no communication.

God does not want us to speak to Him because we have to. He wants us to speak to Him because we want to.

Imagine sitting your child down in a chair in the living room and demanding of them, "Speak to me. Tell me what's up."

What do you suppose your child would tell you?

"Oh, Mom, don't be a ninny," she would probably say. "If I had something to tell you, I'd have told you by now."

That's just exactly what you tell God when you don't talk to Him about your problems. You leave Him out. You ignore His help. Rather stupid thing to do, isn't it, to not let someone help you when that someone has your best interest at heart?

Tell God about your problems with sex. Tell Him about that man who turns you on. Tell Him you want to crawl into bed with that man. Then tell Him it is more important to you to do His will. Could He please lead you away from this situation? Could He please find a way of escape for you?

When you hear an inner voice, if you are surrendered to God, you can assume that the voice is the voice of your spirit which has been in touch with the Holy Spirit.

Again, totally surrender, keep in touch, and you can count on being Spirit led.

Easy Experience

Experience is the best teacher, especially when it is somebody else's lesson you do not need to repeat. It would be terrific if we could all get our experience this way — the easy way.

If you are a Christian reading this material, you probably feel a tug at your "heartstrings." That tug is the Holy Spirit confirming the truth. After all, God wrote His laws on your heart.

If this information is the truth, every time you commit a sexual sin, you feel a godly sorrow. "Godly sorrow brings repentance that leads to salvation and leaves no regret, but worldly sorrow brings death" (2 Cor. 7:10).

God does are not require you to live by "mechanically obeying" a set of laws. He asks you to live in harmony with the Spirit (conscience) given to you.

Paul tells about this struggle with sin. He finally found the solution in Romans 7:6-25 and 8:1-4. Read these Scriptures in the Living Bible and note much of what follows is paraphrased from these passages.

Paul tells us we need no longer worry about the Jewish laws and customs. As a Christian, you "died" to the law. Now you can "really serve God; *not in the old way, mechanically obeying a set of rules,* but in a new way (with all of your hearts and minds)."

The laws of God are not evil. Of course not! But the law has shown us how we are to love one another. The law shows us our sins. We would not know some of the things we do are wrong if the law did not exist.

Paul points out that when you know something is evil and you dwell on those thoughts, it arouses all kinds of forbidden desires within you! "Only if there were no laws to break would there be no sinning."

Paul felt fine when he did not understand what the law really demanded. When he learned the truth, he realized he was, indeed, a sinner, doomed to die.

So as far as Paul was concerned, the good law was supposed to show him the way to live a good life and show him the way to achieve contentment. Instead, he discovered that as far as God was concerned, he deserved the death penalty.

Remember the story about the woman whose brother-in-law had molested his own daughters? Remember how disgusted she was? As far as she was concerned, that sin was bad enough that he deserved the death penalty. Can we assume this is how God feels toward the sins in our lives? Would you hurt your mother by doing something you know would hurt her? Then why would you hurt your Creator in the same way?

Paul said sin fooled him by taking the good laws of God and using them against him, to make him guilty of death. In other words, if I decided I would die anyway because of my sin, would there be any use of even trying? If I felt it was too hard, wouldn't I just give it up? Might as well live it up. Might as well go for the gusto.

The law itself was wholly right and good. But how can that be? Didn't the law cause our doom? How then can it be good? The law is good, then, and the trouble is not there, but with you, in your sin nature. *You don't understand yourself. You really want to do what is right, but you can't.* If you don't want to do what you are doing, odds are it is the sin nature in you, not your spirit. Your spirit has already been redeemed.

Now, you do what you don't want to do — what you hate. You know perfectly well what you are doing is wrong. *Your bad conscience proves that you agree with the laws you break.* But you can't help yourself, because you are no longer doing it. It is sin inside you that is stronger than you are that makes you do evil things. You know you are rotten through and through so far as your old sinful nature is concerned. No matter which way you turn **YOU** can't make yourself do right. You want to, but you can't. When you want to do good, you don't; and when you try not to do wrong, you do it anyway.

If you are doing what you don't want to, it is plain the trouble lies in the sin nature that still has you in its evil grasp. It seems to be a fact of life that when you want to do what is right, inevitably you do wrong. You love to do God's will so far as your new nature is concerned, but there is something else deep within you, in your lower nature, that is at war with your mind and wins the fight and makes you a slave to the sin that is still within you. In your mind you want to be God's willing servant but you find yourself instead enslaved still to sin.

Your life in Christ tells you to do right, but the old nature inside you still loves to sin. What a terrible predicament!

Who will free you from your slavery to this deadly lower nature? Thank God! It has been done by Jesus Christ our Lord. He has set you free. Note the tense of this sentence is past tense — it has already been taken care of.

So there is now no condemnation awaiting you because you belong to Christ Jesus. For the power of the life-giving Spirit — and this power is yours through Christ Jesus — has freed you from the vicious circle of sin and death.

You are not saved from sin's grasp by knowing the commandments of God, because you cannot and do not keep them. God put into effect a different plan to save you. He sent His own Son in a human body like ours — except that ours are sinful — and destroyed sin's control over you by giving himself as a sacrifice for your sins.

"So now you can obey God's laws *if you follow after the Holy Spirit and no longer obey the evil nature within you.*" (The above text is a paraphrase of Romans 7 and 8; this specific text is Romans 7:25.)

Keep following your sin nature and you are lost and will perish. Through the power of the Holy Spirit *you* can crush your sin nature and its evil deeds, and you will live. You crush your sinful nature, not God, but you crush it with God's help. It becomes easier and easier to do when you are led by the Holy Spirit. "For all who are led by the Spirit of God are sons of God" (Rom. 8:14).

The good news is that everything is permissible or lawful to you as a Christian, but not everything is beneficial. You are not to be mastered by anything. You are not subject to the law. You are to, of your own free will, live willingly by the law. God insists that we love. The law is love in action.

Additionally, we are to place nothing in a position to take precedence over our relationship with the Lord. If a habit, like sex — or drugs or cigarettes or alcohol or food — is mastering us, it has become a lord in our lives. God is a jealous God. Your life brings you nothing but dissatisfaction and unhappiness when you flaunt God's laws. You may have fun, for a time, but lasting contentment eludes you.

Experience tells me the conscience is the key. The word itself and its meaning bears this out. The word "conscience" derives from a Latin word *conscire* meaning "con-science" or "with knowing." There is also a word *conscientia* which means "a moral sense of knowledge." The word "conscience" from a Greek word *suneidesis*, which means "knowing or to know the truth."

Even Charlie Manson's girls, who participated in the Tate-La Bianca murders in the late sixties, reported having a conscience. Patricia Krenwinkle reported she chased down the Folgers woman and stabbed her close to 20 times. When Tex Watson sent her to the pool house to slay anyone there, her conscience stopped her at the door. She refused to follow through. The next night, though, at the La Bianca home, she reported that she had become numb. She stabbed Mr. La Bianca with a fork dozens of times, leaving it in him as a "witchy" reminder.

If you have a conscience, be thankful. It means you are still connected. If you do not have a conscience, if you are numb . . . I leave the conclusion to you.

* * *

One thing frustrates me. I cannot explain this personal relationship with Jesus in human terms. This is one experience you cannot get the easy way. I cannot explain the power. I cannot explain my faith. You must experience this first hand. You must ask for it.

About sex, it is possible to learn from the experience of others. It is my prayer that you learn from my experience about this sin. This is experience the easy way. It is my prayer that you suffer none of the consequences.

One broken heart is a lesson learned, but wouldn't you rather it be my heart and not yours?

Peace of mind is a thing to seek after.

Which would you prefer? — a broken heart or peace of mind.

One night I was speaking with a friend, Dana, about this issue. A tall striking lady with blonde curls feathering around her lovely face, she is a model Christian, but a lonely one. We were sitting at the table at her home in south Tulsa one Thanksgiving day discussing, as usual, men.

"You cannot convince me it is wrong to have sex outside of marriage if you really love the person," she said, anger dripping in her voice tone. "God understands. Sex is His idea. . . . Besides, if you plan to marry, what's the big deal? In God's sight, we're already married."

"True, you are one in His sight," I replied. "And I believe God does understand and is merciful. . . . Have you ever analyzed what makes you happy?"

"Not in detail," Dana replied, as she set the table with the last of the vegetables for dinner.

"I have. Remember how Charles professed to be a Christian?"

"I remember."

"Remember how I believed we would eventually marry? He said he loved and wanted to marry me. I had every reason to believe, didn't I?"

"Yes, I guess you did."

"Remember when he disappeared?

"How could I forget?"

"When he left my heart was mutilated."

"I know. It was awful watching you go through it. I didn't know how to help."

"As bad as that was, can you imagine how it would be to *be* left at the altar? Do you think the dumpee would do things differently if they had known the outcome beforehand?"

As the if the revelation finally made sense to her, anger left Dana like hydrogen expelled from a popped balloon. "You're probably right," Dana said as she plopped down in a chair to await the baking dinner rolls.

"Don't you think it would affect future relationships? Frankly, I never want to go through the heartbreak again."

We both agreed that a broken heart is a risk we take if we choose to indulge. Although it would hurt even if you did not engage in sex, the "pain factor" increased exponentially.

Ask around. You find people everywhere staying out of committed relationships because of the fear of that pain.

Conversely, many others are skipping from relationship to relationship, adding partners the way some people add to their wardrobe, like they are trying each person on for size.

I don't know why it is easier on a man's conscience for him to mess around, but apparently it is. A man might indulgently have sexual relations with women who hold no threat to his freedom or his heart. He apparently can justify this behavior.

And many men say exactly what they think you want to hear in order to get you in bed. Their words don't mean anything, they have just learned what to say.

One man I dated twice is a perfect example. John is an ordained minister as well as a Vietnam vet counselor. John had only been born-again for four years, but the Lord was using him in mighty ways. John was also a former marine, having earned just about every conceivable medal and award possible for a marine to earn. He had the confidence women love. He dressed well with every pleat rigidly pressed and smooth surfaces spit polished to mirror finish. John spoke in a deep booming voice. He had much going for him.

John, definitely a ladies man, knew what to say and when to say it. He rained compliments on me. He sent me sweet, mushy cards. We spoke for hours by phone. John would pick me up for a date in his fire-engine red Dodge Stealth, which he told me over and over again was a $40,000 automobile. I guess he assumed I wanted to know. He took me to the finest restaurants in the city. He would open my doors, serve my drinks, order my meals. It was pleasant, indeed.

I could see our ministries melding. I could see a future serving the Lord together.

Oh, there were some things about him that seemed slightly off, like the gun he carried in his glove compartment. Supposedly he was a former sheriff's deputy and needed a gun when dealing with vets whose psychotic behavior might surface.

The final straw, the thing that turned me off — after I told him my feelings on sex, explaining this book, John said, "I can't see us going out for very long without having sex." Even had he not said that, everything he said was so canned, it was like he used the same spiel on every woman he dated. Sincere? Doubtful.

It made me realize . . . I would almost prefer a man to be inept than to have him so smooth it is apparent his experience is legion.

John was an interesting man. He had quite a story to tell. I wanted to stay friends with him just to keep up with what he was doing. I could see him going great places. In fact, I could see him in an important television outreach if he continued to follow God.

Friendship did not materialize. Not after I laid the ground rules. I guess he found me to be one of the "goofy women" he said were everywhere in the church. Maybe I am goofy, but I'd rather be goofy and happy than live by his standards and suffer the consequences. Besides, it's men like him who make us Christian women goofy. They talk out of both sides of their mouths. No thanks!

Many Christian women I am finding do offer themselves as a sacrifice on the altar of their own physical and emotional needs.

I'll never forget one night our Sunday school class had a dance. One woman, Terri, was very outgoing, almost to the point of being obnoxious. You had to like her. She was so much fun. A buxom lady in her mid-thirties, she had been divorced a little over a year when she was elected president of a giant singles' Sunday school class.

Terri experienced something common to the newly divorced . . . the crazies. Terri manifested this divorce stage in the extreme. The night of the dance she was to demonstrate it in a way that left a lasting impression on me. Because of that evening, I almost never went back to that church again.

What happened? Terri took me by the hand, walked me around the room, pointed out men along the way, and rated each one she had slept with. These men attended the same church. Thank God, that was several years ago and these people and that church have since become a great deal more spiritual.

There are plenty of "Christian" men to take advantage of needy "Christian" women. Terri was obviously needy. And Terri is definitely a Christian, though a carnal one. Unfortunately, she sacrificed her own long-range happiness. She now has a reputation. She can't take it back. She wants to, but she can't.

You may defend a loving sexual relationship with the justification "We are as good as married in God's eyes anyway."

There is difficulty in using this justification. How do you distinguish between that person who will definitely commit to you and the person who wants to use you?

How can you tell which relationship will eventually lead to holy matrimony?

And again, if you knew he would leave you at the end, would you do what you did in the beginning?

Not so long ago we had sexual freedom according to society standards. *Playboy's* philosophy was to have as many sexual partners as it is possible to have. Of course, now that he has experienced practically every woman, and I understand every man he has desired, Hugh Hefner opted to marry and have a family. Wonder why! Loneliness? Does that mean his philosophy failed him? I know it has generally failed multiplied millions of the "lovelorn." People want love.

Notice how quickly sexual freedom disappeared? Even before AIDS, people were discovering how shallow sport sex can be.

Yet still there are commitment-phobic men.

Dave Barry, a columnist who writes for the Knight-Ridder newspaper service and creator of the television sitcom "Dave," writes about these commitment-phobic men:

> Today we're going to explore the mysterious topic of How Guys Think, which has baffled women in general, and the editors of Cosmopolitan magazine in particular for thousands of years. The big question, of course, is: How come guys never call? After successful dates, I mean. . . . at the end of the evening he says, quote, "Can I call you?" And you, interpreting this to mean, "Can I call you?" answer: "Sure!"
>
> The instant you say this, the guy's body starts to dematerialize . . . he has vanished entirely into the mysterious Guy Bermuda Triangle, where whole squadrons of your dates have disappeared over the years, never to be heard from again. . . .
>
> There's nothing wrong with you. In fact, you should interpret the behavior . . . as kind of a guy compliment to you. Because when the guy asks you if he can call you, what he's really asking you, in Guy Code, is will you marry him. Yes. See, your basic guy is into a straight-ahead, bottom-line kind of thought process that does not work nearly as well with the infinitely subtle complexities of human relationships as it does with calculating how much gravel is needed to cover a given driveway. So, here's what the guy is thinking: If he calls you, you'll go out again,

and you'll probably have another great time, and
so on until the only possible OPTION will be to
get married. This is classic Guy Logic.[13]

I have a point in quoting this very instructional material. A
man will sometimes stay away from a woman if he fears a long-
term commitment. Why? Because he doesn't want a long-term
commitment.

For selfish reasons, many men want a woman who will not
demand strings. Remember the male friend I mentioned earlier
who is like the stallion roaming amongst the mares? He says he
really does not want to marry because he is too selfish. There are
women willing to allow him the blessing of sex without the responsibility God planned would go with that blessing.

God *might* consider it no worse to have sex with someone
you love than to tell a white lie. Like a parent setting guidelines
for the child, God does not want to spoil your fun.

When faced with your man and temptation, remember . . .
God loves you and wants your happiness more than that man
could ever love you or want your happiness.

Understand the difference between immediate gratification
versus eternal rewards. Temptations are instantaneous and immediate. The easiest route is immediate gratification.

If I knew when I started smoking what I know now, I would
suffer without gratifying my curiosity. I knew I would not go to
hell for smoking . . . I'd just smell like it. And quitting was hell
on earth. If my ex-husband had known when he started drinking
that gratifying his desire to "fit in" would end in his "checking
out," I'm sure he would make the necessary changes.

If we develop patience to suffer through the situations causing temptation, eventually we receive what God promised.

So, when you are faced with being alone with that man,
remember God is willing to help. *And with His help*, remaining
celibate can be your chosen lifestyle.

What can you learn the easy way?

What can you learn from my experience?

Without the biblically sanctioned marriage commitment,
sex is an amusement park for the body and a hellhole for the
soul.

Your Conscience Guide

A motto I heard recently says it plainly enough: "When in doubt, chicken out." Below are situations that may arise. What would you do?

1) Situation: In a club with friends after a nice dinner, you feel uneasy in the pit of your stomach. You are NOT comfortable, and you don't know why.

Solution: It is time to leave. You will feel a peace in your spirit when you allow the Holy Spirit to lead you.

2) Situation: You want a cigarette, but covertly you glance around. Is anyone from the church watching?

Solution: If it bothers you for someone from the church to find you smoking, it is your conscience speaking. And the conscience is the Holy Spirit. Make a determination to be willing to become willing for God to work His way in your life. Ask God to help you. When you walk in the Spirit, the result is peace.

3) Situation: Sitting at a table with some friends, they begin to gossip about someone. You find yourself joining in, but you do not feel right about it.

Solution: When walking in the Spirit, you know it is not right to bare false witness. Even if telling the truth, does it edify, exhort, or encourage?

4) Situation: Speaking with a friend you find yourself beginning to argue. You realize the outcome of this disagreement means that you will win the argument, but might lose the friend.

Solution: With the Spirit you become a peacemaker and long-suffering. Winning is no longer the issue — love is.

5) Situation: You discover you have walked out of the grocery store with too much change.

Solution: You immediately take the change back and correct the situation. When you walk in the Spirit, you do not steal.

6) Situation: Working for a company for many years, you take an item home from time to time. The item is at your house when you leave the company and no one says anything to you about it. Should you return the item?

Solution: When you walk in the Spirit, you return the item. You do not walk in greed.

7) Situation: At the movie there is a sex scene. This is some-

thing you have seen before. But this time you cannot tolerate watching it any longer.

Solution: When you walk in the Spirit, you do not walk in lust. You either leave the movie entirely or walk out during scene hoping another will not occur.

These are a few situations that come to mind, but there are many more.

Go and walk in peace.

Chapter 14

Step #4 —
To Hell with
the Devil!

Know your enemy and what he wants. Send him home.

Satan has a plan. He wants to put enough pressure on you so you give up. He wants you to toss your Bible out the window. He wants you to believe the Word does not work. The adversary comes immediately to steal any new revelation you receive.

"When anyone hears the message about the kingdom and does not understand it, the evil one comes and snatches away what was sown in his heart. This is the seed sown along the path" (Matt. 13:19).

Isn't this what happened to Thelma? Remember? Right after she read the first draft of this book her ex-boyfriend resurfaced.

Well, to hell with the devil.

Stand firm, steadfast, knowing that the Lord will help you. Set your face like flint. "Because the Sovereign Lord helps me, I will not be disgraced. Therefore have I set my face like flint, and I know I will not be put to shame" (Isa. 50:7).

In his book, *Putting Your Angels to Work,* Norvel Hayes talks about pleasing God, about "caring more what God thinks of you than you do about what man thinks of you." He says:

> In love you explain to your loved ones what you are doing and why you believe God wants you to do it. But then, whether they agree or not, you listen to the voice of God, rather than the voice of man. That's faith.

The following paragraph from his book is especially significant:

> God is a spirit. He lives inside each believer. God, the Holy Spirit, who inhabits your earthly body does not think any differently from God the Father who lives in heaven. Father, Son, and Holy Ghost all think and speak in line with God's Word. *Whatever the Word of God says, that's the way it is. You might as well make up your mind to accept that truth and learn to live by it!* Jesus said that those who worship God must worship Him in spirit and in truth. That is, in word and deed.[14]

If you will do that, if you continually worship and praise the Lord in spirit and in truth (spiritually *and physically),* then he will see to it that all your needs are met. "But seek first his kingdom and his righteousness, and all these things will be given to you as well" (Matt. 6:33).

Do you think trials and tests come your way because you are not "good enough"? The opposite more likely is the case. It is because you are "good enough" that tests come.

Have you asked, "Why me, Lord?" Simple! God has a plan for you. God sent you to accomplish His purpose. Satan does not want you to succeed. When you come close, Satan pulls out his big guns.

How does the devil work when it comes to sex? Elementary! He wants you to decide you cannot live a life that will be pleasing to God. He wants you to consider yourself condemned.

Condemnation comes from Satan. "For the accuser of our brothers, who accuses them before our God day and night, has been hurled down" (Rev. 12:10).

Conviction comes from God. "Godly sorrow brings repentance that leads to salvation and leaves no regret, but worldly sorrow brings death" (2 Cor. 7:10).

What's the difference?

Condemnation suggests punishment and damnation. With it comes feelings of hopelessness. Your desire to change is thwarted by your perception that it is worthless effort. If you are continuing in sexual sin, this may be your feeling. Sex outside of marriage goes against your belief system, but you do it anyway, believing to live otherwise is not possible.

Conviction uplifts and edifies. Conviction brings with it a probability of betterment. You want to change. You understand God's love for you and His reasons for wanting you to be holy.

The devil does not ever want you to understand this and he will do everything in his power to keep this information from you.

You can live a holy life. You can find things to do to fill your time. You can choose to make a difference in your community rather than in your bed.

One of the best ways of defeating the devil is by praising God. As a parent, I'm sure you enjoy hearing some words of thanks from your child once in a while.

I've noticed, too, even in praise, it seems God has meant this for our good. Due to family commitments, I changed churches, no longer attending one church where we raised our hands during praise and worship time. The next church I attended, the music was staid and old fashioned, and everybody sang while holding hymnals. At another church, after a two-hour service where we praised with enthusiasm and raised hands, I left refreshed. When I left the one-hour service, I was ready for a nap. So I wonder, did God know I would physically feel better after praising Him? I dare you to raise your hands and sing and not feel better.

Worship is your weapon, the way you send the devil to

hell. What you worship, you listen to. You allow yourself to be mastered by that which you worship. That's how the devil tempted Jesus. He wanted Jesus to worship him and sin against God, and he wants you to do the same. For many, he is succeeding.

It started in the Garden of Eden when Satan convinced Adam and Eve to listen to him. As a result, they lost heaven on earth.

Again, from the book, *Putting Your Angels to Work*, by Norvel Hayes, he relates this about worship:

> *Did you know that when you sin, what you are actually doing is siding with Satan against God?* Like Adam and Eve, you are taking the word of a fallen angel rather than standing on the Word of Almighty God, Maker of Heaven and Earth. *To choose Satan is to serve Satan. In essence, when you give your body to sin you are falling down and worshipping the devil.*[15]

Ouch! Did that ever hit home.

"Oh, no, I'd never do that!"

Well, if you wouldn't worship the devil, then why do you listen to him *and do what he wants you to do* instead of listening to God and doing what pleases Him? What is worship but obedience and service?

You see, there are two spiritual fathers in this world. Every day of your life you must make a choice of which one you will serve. Either you serve the Father of life, or you serve the father of liars! The one you choose is the one you will serve. The choice is up to you.

So what do you do when you feel yourself getting aroused? Is it possible to remember what might happen? Could you make that a prayer? That you remember?

If you remember nothing else, *"In essence, when you give your body to sin you are falling down and worshipping the devil."* How, then, can you expect God's blessings?

God's Exchange System

There is a formula for sending the devil home:

So give yourselves humbly to God. Resist the devil and he will flee from you. And when you draw close to God, God will draw close to you. Wash your hands, you sinners, and let your hearts be filled with God alone and make them pure and true to Him. Let there be tears for the wrong things you have done. Let there be sorrow and sincere grief. Let there be sadness instead of laughter, and gloom instead of joy. Then when you realize your worthlessness before the Lord, He will lift you up, encourage and help you (James 4:7-10;TLB).

Here is the formula:
1) *Your Part — Draw near to God.*
God's Part — He will draw near to you.
The more you read His Word, the more you know Him. The more you know Him, the more you know what He wants. The more you know what He wants, the closer you will be to Him.

2) *Your Part — Resist the devil.*
God's Part — He will make the devil flee from you.
When you resist, the devil will flee from you. You resist him by following the promptings of your spirit. You resist him by drawing closer to God. You resist him by using the Word as a sword against him.

3) *Your Part — Confess your sins.*
God's Part — He will forgive your sins.
Confess your sins or wash your hands. This does not say you won't be required to wash your hands again and again and again.

4) *Your Part — Fill your heart with God.*
God's Part — To direct your path.
When you are full of God, you will not be sinning against your fellow man.

5) *Your Part — Be sorry.*
God's Part — He will show you how to love.
Be sorry for the wrong things you do, because your wrongs

probably hurt someone else. Do not be sorry only because you got caught and might suffer punishment. God knows your sincerity. Rather, be sorry because you have wronged your brother, you have not shown love. Jesus tells us that if we love, we fulfill the law. The law is God's way of trying to explain to puny man how to love. Be sorry, too, for hurting God, just as you would be sorry if you hurt your earthly parent.

6) *Your Part — Humble yourself.*
God's Part — He will lift you up.

When you humble yourself before the Lord, His Word says He will lift you up. What a promise!

In other words, we are responsible for making the right decision about our sex life. If you continue in an affair with someone, you are not submitting yourself to God, but rather to that man. You are laying down with the devil. You are believing him.

How can it be that Jesus is the author of our faith then? How can you still make mistakes? Simple. He may write the play, but if we don't use the words, if we ad lib, how would the play end? We truly understand His authorship and His development only as submitted Christians willing to turn away from sin, willing to stick with His script.

When we submit to man in this way, God's says we are turning our backs on Him and despising Him (Isa. 1:3-4). Will He help those who despise Him? Will you be happy if you do not have His help? We "walk bent-backed beneath [our] load of guilt." Do you feel that burden at times?

At church one day I met Tony. About 50 years of age, he grew up Catholic in New Hampshire. He received his salvation in 1984.

At that time Tony lived with a lady. Immediately upon his conversion, his spirit was renewed and he felt the weight of his guilt. Within three months of his conversion, he walked away from the relationship.

His girlfriend did not understand. Not at all. She wanted to marry Tony, but Tony did not want to marry her. He had been using her. She was convenient. Eventually, Tony led the woman to the Lord. She met another Christian man, and they are now happily married.

Before his conversion, Tony experienced years of depression. He went for counseling twice weekly for four years. The day after his conversation Tony walked into the counseling group and told them Jesus had totally healed his depression. What that counseling group tried to do in four years, Jesus did for him in one night.

Their reaction? "Well, that's nice for you, Tony, that you found something that worked for you."

If they only knew.

Was Tony chosen? Were you?

Each Christian has been chosen from the beginning. Everything that happens to us happens just as He decided long ago. "In him we were also chosen, having been predestined according to the plan of him who works out everything in conformity with the purpose of his will, in order that we, who were the first to hope in Christ, might be for the praise of his glory. And you also were included in Christ when you heard the word of truth, the gospel of your salvation. Having believed, you were marked in him with a seal, the promised Holy Spirit" (Eph. 1:11-13;NIV). We are marked as belonging to Christ by the Holy Spirit. "His presence within us is *God's guarantee* that He really will give us all that He promised; and the Spirit's seal upon us means that God has *already* purchased us and that *He guarantees to bring us to himself*" (Eph. 1:14;TLB). I will exchange my will for happiness and His personal guarantee.

If, in fact, you know you are chosen, and if you have God's personal guarantee that He really will give you what He promised to give you, what would be your response? Would it be worth taking some steps that require short-term pain if you could be assured of long-term gain? Can you see God's exchange system? Is it worth it?

Did you know that those of us who do the will of God will praise Him forever, and that includes on judgment day? Logically it does not make sense that we would we praise Him if we were unhappy, does it? Early biblical scholars agree with this assessment. Matthew Henry, who began writing his commentaries in 1704, says:

Where the fear of the Lord rules in the heart there will be a constant conscientious care to keep His commandments, not to talk of them, but to do them; and such have a good understanding. Their obedience is a plain indication of their mind that they do indeed fear God. *We have reason to praise God, to praise him for ever, for putting man into such a fair way of HAPPINESS.*[16]

Isn't that what you want? Happiness? Is it worth some compromises on your part? Do you want make the right decision every time you are faced with a tempting situation?

Yes, if you want better insight and discernment, and are searching for them as you would for lost money or hidden treasure, then wisdom will be given you, and knowledge of God himself; you will soon learn the importance of reverence for the Lord and of trusting him. For the Lord grants wisdom! His ever word is a treasure of knowledge and understanding. He grants good sense to the godly — his saints. He is their shield, protecting them and guarding their pathway. He shows how to distinguish right from wrong, *how to find the right decision every time*. For wisdom and truth will enter the very center of your being filling your life with **joy**" (Prov. 2:3-10;TLB).

We are told specifically how to avoid trouble: "Cling tightly to your faith in Christ, and always *keep your conscience clear, doing what you know is right.* For some people have disobeyed their consciences and have deliberately done what they knew was wrong. It isn't surprising that soon they lost their faith in Christ after defying God like that" (1 Tim. 1:19;TLB).

Are you defying God? The Lord can hear. He isn't deaf. The trouble is, our sins have cut us off from Him. Why take chances? What if I'm right?

Tap into God's strength. "Humble yourselves, therefore, under God's mighty hand, that He may lift you up in due time. Cast all your anxiety on Him because He cares for you. Be self-controlled and alert. Your enemy prowls around like a roaring lion looking for someone to devour. Resist him, standing firm in the faith, because you know that your brothers throughout the world are undergoing the same kind of sufferings. And the God of all grace, who called you to His eternal glory in Christ, after you have suffered a little while, *will himself restore you* and make you strong and steadfast" (1 Pet. 5:6-10;NIV).

So, here's the exchange system:

YOUR PART	GOD'S PART
Humble yourself.	He will lift you up in due time.
Cast all anxiety on Him.	He cares for you.
Resist the enemy.	He will restore you.
Stand firm in the faith.	He will make you strong and steadfast.

Another biblical account illustrates exactly what God wants us to do if we want Him to fight our battles. This is so important I would ask that you pick up your Bible and turn to 2 Chronicles 20. You will find Jehoshaphat in an assembly at the temple. He discusses the forces that were coming against them. In verse 12 you will find the formula: "For we have no power to face this vast army that is attacking us. We do not know what to do, but our eyes are upon you" (NIV).

Here is the formula:

1) Admit you have no power.
2) Admit you do not know what to do.
3) Confess you will look to God for answers.

Later Jehoshaphat tells the assembly that the Lord wants them not to be afraid or discouraged. The Lord wants them to know *"the battle is not yours, but God's."* He instructs them: "Stand quietly and see the incredible rescue operations God will perform for you" (2 Chron. 20:17).

God tells us to let the weak say they are strong (Joel 3:10).

Another excellent exchange. The meek shall inherit the earth (Matt. 5:5). The merciful shall obtain mercy (Matt. 5:7). Those who give will receive (Luke 6:38). Delight yourself in the Lord and He will give you the desires of your heart (Ps. 37:4).

When you begin to read your Bible, you will find all kinds of exchange systems. Who would not want to be a Christian with exchange systems like these available?

Mind Games

Your enemy attacks one way and one way only — through your mind. Constantly thoughts come at you against the knowledge of God. Continuing in sexual sin is against the knowledge of God. Paul tells you how to handle this: "The weapons we fight with are not the weapons of the world. On the contrary, they have divine power to demolish strongholds. WE demolish arguments and every pretension that sets itself up against the knowledge of God and WE take captive every thought to make it obedient to Christ" (2 Cor. 10:4-5;NIV).

Not God, but *we*, ourselves do the demolishing by rejecting the arguments, pretensions, and thoughts that are flung at us by our enemy. We are supposed to think about pleasant things as it says in Philippians 4:8.

God wants to help us, *but He can do nothing until we ask Him.*

A friend, Mary Lou, likened the process to a basketball game. If you play the game alone, you might get lucky and score from time to time. If Jesus is in charge, you win every time. Unfortunately, if you are dribbling the ball you have control. Jesus wants control of the ball so He can win the game for you. "The Lord will fight for you; you need only to be still" (Exod. 14:14). If you don't give Jesus the ball, He cannot do anything for you.

When you do finally pass the ball to Jesus, He will score. He might not do it as quickly as you would like or the way you like or exactly how you tell Him to. He needs to set up His shot. Until you pass Him the ball, He is like the guy standing at the end of the court waving his hands madly in the air. He is trying to get your attention. You'll never know what He will do for you until He has the ball.

You have the keys to the kingdom of heaven to use right here on earth. You simply need to know how to use them. You loose and bind specific things here on earth. You name them. You need to take your sex drive to the Cross. We need to pass that specific ball to Jesus.

The healings in the Bible are good examples of how God works on our behalf. We must ask in order to receive. The Bible says when you need healing, you must do something. If you are sick, *you* are to call the elders of the church (James 5:14).

You do not have because you do not ask God. "If you show special attention to the man wearing fine clothes and say, 'Here's a good seat for you,' but say to the poor man, 'You stand there' or 'Sit on the floor by my feet,' have you not discriminated among yourselves and become judges with evil thoughts?" (James 2:3-4).

In no instance did the Lord heal anyone without first either someone asking or, like the man beside the pool of water, someone saying they wanted to be healed. Jesus never pushed himself on anyone. He was always the gentleman, always awaiting an invitation.

If you do take your sexual sin to Jesus, you can rest assured He will help. Your job is simply to seek His kingdom and His righteousness. You have no righteousness. You could never measure up to what you need. But the loving thing to do, both loving to yourself and to the other person, is to seek to live righteously. If you do, all things you need for living will be given to you. It does not say you earn it. It doesn't say you have to pay for these things. Your job is simply to seek to live in a loving way.

Learning to live this way means you live in 24-hour segments. You won't live yesterday. You cannot take back the sins you committed yesterday. You won't live in tomorrow. Just as an active alcoholic cannot see himself living the rest of his life without a drink, perhaps you cannot see yourself living without sex. But what about today? Can you live without it today?

Mind games, to summarize:

1) You demolish arguments and every pretense that sets itself up against the knowledge

of God. Having sex outside of marriage is against the knowledge of God.

2) You take captive every thought to make it obedient to Christ. If you find yourself getting aroused, switch it off.

3) Ask! Ask God to help you turn it off.

4) Think about things that are true, honest, just, pure, and lovely. If anything good can be found, if there is any virtue, anything you can praise, think of these things. When faced with thoughts of a erotic nature, think about something else.

5) Live in 24-hour segments. If you can give up sex just for today, you can make it a lifetime, one day at a time.

* * *

God promises He will give you whatever you desire with all your heart if you delight in Him (Ps. 37:4). After all, is not God the one who put the desires in your heart? So why would He not fulfill those desires? While God may not do things specifically as you tell Him to do it, it doesn't mean He won't do it.

Garth Brooks has a wonderful song called "Unanswered Prayers." The song is based on true events in his life. In the song he says, "Sometimes I thank God for unanswered prayers." Garth once tried to tell God exactly who he wanted as his wife. He prayed about it many times. God had other plans. Garth married another, but always dreamed of the one that got away . . . until they met again. Garth realized that he really had received the desires of his heart, even though it wasn't exactly as he had planned.

When God does not answer your prayers exactly as you would want them, it means God has something better.

Not dealing with sex, exactly, but dealing with this step is what happened to my friend, Paula. She was going through a divorce and her business dealings were at an all-time low. The condo in which she had invested over $25,000 had not sold. She prayed over and over that God would provide her with the money to stay there. He did not.

Paula and her husband moved into a duplex. They lived there for some time. She was soon to discover that the money she was giving her husband for the rent was being spent, instead, on booze. They were soon evicted.

Paula had no clue what she was going to do.

That's when Paula's mother-in-law came back to town for a visit. She lived in the northeast, but had a second home in Tulsa. She offered Paula the opportunity to live in her home with her daughter rent free while she got back on her feet.

"You should have seen this home," Paula told me. "It was a mansion. Six thousand square feet of a house featured in Tulsa's *Home Beautiful* magazine. And we had maid service five days a week, yard man, and no utilities. I lived there scot-free for four years. That was beyond my wildest dreams."

The truth of the matter is that God wants us to be happy. He wants us to have our desires. Many people don't think so. They believe the devil's lies about God — that he is mean-spirited and vengeful.

You can't read Scripture without finding the same theme over and over. God mentions desires and dreams many times. Your desires are important to God because they will help you achieve your purpose for Him. Listed here are several Scriptures to prove this. You need to get this knowledge deep in your spirit and in your mind.

"Delight yourself in the Lord, and He will *give you the desires of your heart*. Commit your way to the Lord; trust in Him and *He will do this*" (Ps. 37:4-5;NIV).

"Now glory be to God, who by His mighty power at work within me is able to do far more than I would ever dare to ask or even dream of — infinitely beyond my highest prayers, desires, thoughts, or hopes" (Eph. 3:20;NIV).

"The Lord is near to all who call on Him, to all who call on Him in truth. He fulfills the desires of those who fear Him; He hears their cry and saves them" (Ps. 145:18-19;NIV).

"Your kingdom is an everlasting kingdom and Your dominion endures through all generations. The Lord is faithful to all His promises and loving toward all He has made" (Ps. 145:13;NIV).

"May He give me the desire of my heart and make all my plans succeed. I will shout for joy when I am victorious [notice this says 'when I am victorious,' not 'if'] and will lift up my banners in the name of our God. May the Lord grant all my requests" (Ps. 20:4-5;NIV).

"And without faith it is impossible to please God, because anyone who comes to Him must believe that He exists and that He *rewards* those who earnestly seek Him" (Heb. 11:6;NIV).

Manipulate your mind by memorizing this simple formula:

Faith = believing that what you cannot see will come to pass.
Fear = believing that what you cannot see will come to pass.

What do you see? Do you see your desires coming to pass? You may say, "I don't have enough faith for that." If you have enough faith to pray about something, that may very well be enough faith. Your lack of faith will not nullify God's faithfulness.

Do what the Word tells you to do, and you can stand on what the Word says. He watches over His Word to perform it (Jer. 1:12) and His Word does not return to Him void (Is. 55:11). The Lord will accomplish that which concerns you (Ps. 138:8). Note this says the Lord will accomplish these things — not you. You may be required to do something, but God will accomplish what needs to be done. You do the leg work. He will do it, He will bring about the change.

Having faith in God pleases Him, and He rewards those who diligently seek Him.

Remember Christ's love for us? "That Christ may dwell in your hearts by faith; that you, being rooted and grounded in love, may be able to comprehend with all saints what is the breadth, and length, and depth, and height; and to know the love of Christ which passes knowledge, that you might be filled with all the fullness of God. Now unto Him that is able to do exceeding abundantly above all that we ask or think, according to *power that works in us*" (Eph. 3:17-20;KJV).

Change your mind. Manipulate your thinking. Decide to believe you have God's help and God's power, the same power that raised Jesus from the dead.

Of course, God is not a drive-up God. He will not allow you to pop in, place your order, expect to get it quickly, and then move on. His desires become your desires. And then if you ask anything according to His will, you can be assured He hears you. If He hears you, you can be sure you have the petitions you desire of Him. In His time.

Here's a mind game you might call the "face like flint" game:

1) *You tell* your mind what to think.
2) *You tell* your mouth what to say.
3) *You tell* your body what to do.
4) *You think* what the Word says to think.
5) *You say* what the Word says to say.
6) *You do* what the Word says to do.
7) *You make the Bible, the Word of God, your final authority.*

Manipulate your mind.

Play games with your thoughts.

Rely on God and He will direct your path.

Chapter 15

Step #5 — God's "Believe It or Not!"

Real faith is trusting in the midst of failure and continuing to trust in the midst of fortune.

No way to please God without it, without realizing that nothing is impossible for Him.

God is an "either-or" God. You are either for Him or against Him, as we are told in Matthew 12:30. You either choose death or life. About faith or fear? Is it also true that you either have faith or you have fear? YES!!! You cannot live in faith as long as you allow yourself to live in fear. God does not give fear. He's a good giver, giving power, love, and a sound mind.

Remember the formula? Faith = believing that what you cannot see will come to pass. Fear = believing that what you cannot see will come to pass.

Satan is a bad giver, sending frightening thoughts. His purpose? To get you to dwell on them, using his usual method to threaten you — your mind.

Regarding sex, how does Satan frighten you? Isn't it with loneliness?

Gene and Mandy are a perfect example of one way fear of loneliness manifests itself in the single scene. Gene is a pencil-thin, rather short, average-looking man whose only distinguishing characteristic is that he is well dressed. Gene definitely would not stand out in a crowd. Conversely, Mandy's strawberry blonde tresses billow upon her shoulders, a collection of decorative belts adorn and emphasize her tiny waist, and her long legs would turn any head. Gene and Mandy met one night at a local dance club.

Appearing in Sunday school together the next Sunday, they were recognized as a couple. Quickly they allowed themselves to swept away into an impetuous marriage.

The engagement, attended by members of the class, occurred at the same dance club where they first met. It was Mandy's birthday. Gene carefully planned his proposal with flowers and a musical dedication oozing with romance. Down on one knee in the center of the dance floor, his cowboy hat in hand, Gene pledged his troth. Mandy said yes. With a kiss, they sealed the deal.

Now, three years later, it appears the marriage was simply a business arrangement for Mandy. During the past year Mandy's ex-husband sued and won custody of their children. Mandy blames Gene. Not because of the children. Mandy called later and chewed Gene up one side and down the other. The children were furious with her because she decided to divorce him. The kids loved Gene.

While Mandy had custody, she was happy to be married to Gene, obviously for financial reasons. But the moment she no longer needed him or his income to "bring up baby," she was gone. When she left, she broke the heart of a good man.

Did Mandy marry Gene strictly out of fear? Was she so afraid of raising the children alone that she chose to marry a man she did not love?

Melissa, a lovely woman of 40, has an adorable figure, a

pert smile, and flowing blonde hair. Her wholesome, girl-next-door appeal would catch the eye of many a man. Adding to her appeal, she is unencumbered with children. She has no fear of the financial concerns that plague many single women her age.

"The most difficult thing I have ever done in my life," she shared with me privately one morning in church, "is to stop having sex. One day my husband was there and everything was fine. The next day, my husband was gone, and immediately sex was transgression."

Divorced for two years, Melissa dated only one person. "He left after three months because I was too religious for him. I would not go to bed with him, so he's gone. Is that the way it is always going to be?"

Will Melissa give up? Will she decide it's too hard? What if she decides to give in? Will she suffer consequences? Will her fear of not having a man be more powerful than her fear of hurting God?

In a recent survey of a denominational church in town, it was discovered that more than 80 percent of those questioned had engaged in an affair within a year of their divorce. All said it was against their values.

If it is against their values, why are they doing what they are doing? Are they afraid of marriage? Are they afraid of love? If they are afraid of these things, does that not mean they are living in fear and not in faith? Have they forgotten to put God in the equation?

If Melissa were to give in, she would be doing things against God's best, against what God has provided for her. What do you suppose will happen? Or should I ask, what do you believe the odds are that Melissa would have some sort of negative repercussion?

Do you become fainthearted when faced with temptations, trials, and tribulations? Do circumstances seem so demanding that you overload? Then think about Christ's patience as men did terrible things to Him. You haven't struggled against sin and temptation until you sweat great drops of blood (Luke 22:44).

* * *

Have you ever noticed how you will get the legs knocked right out from under you just when things are going well? Doesn't it seem that you end up in circumstances that are beyond your control?

Do you feel like Moses at the Red Sea?

Why do you suppose that happens? If you were God, and you wanted to get your child's attention, if you could fix it so they would have to come to you for help, would you do it? What if your child went to someone else instead? How would that make you feel?

What do you do when you are at the Red Sea? Do you turn to God? Or do you turn to man? Man may help you, but are you making the effort, or does God have them call you? Do you rely on yourself and your own ability to get yourself out of a situation? Or do you ask God in prayer to give you the answers when you need them — and then wait for them no matter what the circumstances?

In my case with Charles, when he left I assumed responsibility. I tried to bring him back with love letters, sweet cards, and pleasant phone calls. I tried to convince him with reasoning that I was perfect for him. Certainly he was sick to death of me. When these ideas to win him back came to mind I believed they were God's promptings. Perhaps they were. Perhaps this was God's way of maneuvering me to a lesson learned. I did not realize it was a Red Sea.

God allowed me to suffer the consequences of my actions, to suffer the pain of lost love. God instructed me this way because he could not get me to listen any other way.

In retrospect, I am thankful God took the time to instruct me. After all, would I take the time to train someone else's child? When God punished me by allowing me to suffer the consequences of sleeping with Charles, it proved to me that I am really His child. Had I escaped the pain of the affair, odds are I would not really be His child after all. "If you are not disciplined (and everyone undergoes discipline), then you are illegitimate children and not true sons" (Heb. 12:8).

Remembering what it was like prior to my conversion, I know that I was not bothered by this sin the way I am now bothered by this sin after my salvation. After all, have you ever heard of a daughter who was loved by her father but never corrected?

Did your earthly father punish you? Did you respect him for doing so? What would you think of an earthly father who allowed you to do anything at all you wanted to do? You would say that such a father did not love his child.

Realizing that our Heavenly Father loves us enough to correct us, perhaps we should all the more *"cheerfully* submit to His training *so that we can begin to really live "* (Heb. 12:9). Would you really begin to live if you had problems weighing you down? Would you really begin to live if you were happy and carefree? What do you suppose this Scripture means by "begin to really live"?

Our earthly fathers train us for a few brief years, doing the best they know how. But "God's correction is always right and **for our best good,** that we may share His holiness" (Heb. 12:10). Being punished is not fun while it is happening — *it hurts!* But *afterwards* we can see the result, a quiet growth in grace and character.

Recently I had lunch with Terese Hall, who is a counselor for a Counseling Care Associates in Tulsa. She and the director, Dr. Ed Decker, an ordained minister, speak all over the country to Christian singles' organizations. Their topic? "Sexual Sanity in a Sensuous Society." One of the lessons they emphasize is the need to make friends of the opposite sex. We need to know people as human beings, not simply objects of lust. And if you know someone as a friend, would you want to hurt them?

Remember the man named Scott who said women wanted him to make a pass or they would not believe he was interested? I wonder . . . if he really cared for women as he would care for his best friend or his sister, would he bed them knowing he would soon be gone? If he knew he would cause them pain, would he allow them to coerce him into sex? If Scott really had a Christian attitude of love, he would consider the long-range effects of this activity, not simply the immediate gratification.

In fact I heard a report on the radio just recently that they had done a study of sexually active women. They discovered that the more active a woman was, the more men she had been to bed with, the more she felt used by them. So, those who are claiming to enjoy this sexual freedom are being hurt by it. My immediate response when I heard this was, "Duh. . . ." I can't imagine why they're just now figuring this out. So even though men may believe a woman doesn't get hurt because she's been with many other men, even then he is wrong.

We are to look after each other so that not one person will fail to *find God's best blessings.* And we are specifically told to *"watch out that no one becomes involved in sexual sin* — or becomes careless about God" (Heb. 12:16).

Paul gives the example of Esau, who traded His rights as the oldest son for a single meal. Afterwards, when he wanted those rights back again, it was too late, even though he wept bitter tears of repentance. Remember Melinda who was dumped by Jack? Do you think she would have wanted to "take back her rights again" after Jack left? So, remember, and be careful because odds are the man will not treat you like a sister.

"So see to it that you obey Him who is speaking to you" (Heb. 12:25). Do you feel a confirmation in your Spirit that what is written here is right? You realize, of course, that it is the Holy Spirit. Then obey Him who is speaking to you.

As mentioned previously, you do not have a vote about your correction or discipline by God. In Isaiah 55:8-9 we are told this: " 'For my thoughts are not your thoughts, neither are your ways my ways,' declares the Lord. 'As the heavens are higher than the earth, so are my ways higher than your ways and my thoughts than your thoughts.' "

God does what He wants to do when He wants to do it.

What is hard to grasp is that God is with you, really there with you, even during the failures. When you get it that these are your "tutoring times," then maybe you can hang on, wade through, and come out the other side with more faith. That is, after all, what He wants.

Do you believe?

Chapter 16

Step #6 — The Choice That Brings the Angels Out to Play!

Choose to use the Word of God.

Choices! Always choices! Which choice do you make? What can you expect if you choose life? When you follow your conscience, do you realize that choosing life is what you are doing? When Jesus was tempted He fought off Satan with the Word of God. Then the devil left Him, and angels came to minister to Him (Matt. 4:11).

When you face temptation, use Scripture to fight it. That is exactly what Christ did at His temptation. He said "It is written . . ." every time Satan tempted Him. Then take this Scripture, personalize it as I have here, and say aloud. "It is written the Lord God will help me; therefore, I shall not be confounded: therefore, I have set my face like flint, and I know I shall not be ashamed" (Isa. 50:7). Upon examination of the passage in Matthew regarding the temptation of Christ, note that when Jesus said to Satan, "Get thee hence," Satan left.

Following your conscience is choosing life. Using the Word is choosing life. The angels come out to minister to you.

Disregarding your conscience is choosing death. Material goods may come, but not peace of mind. Guess who comes to minister to you! Angels, all right. Fallen angels, commonly called demons.

What happened when I choose to follow my conscience? Once I made the decision to stop having sex with Charles, I felt the angels ministering to me. I choose to live this lifestyle, NOT because I am mindlessly following a set of rules. I choose this in order to live in the revelation God gave me. The revelation? What sin is to God, and what sin eventually does to me, the believer.

Before I became totally sold on God's Word, I bought into the standards and morals of society. In doing so, I condemned myself. I chose death without even knowing it. Maybe not a death of my spirit, because as a Christian I have salvation. Certainly the death of my hopes of seeing the kingdom of God here on earth.

The angels who came to minister to me when I chose to leave sex alone helped me find the truth — not only in the Word, but through other people, through writings, and through revelations that came to me in prayer.

Second Peter 2:1-2 (TLB) sounds very much like the situation today and it warns: "But there were false prophets, too, in those days, just as there will be false teachers among you. They will cleverly tell their lies about God, turning against even their Master who bought them; but their's will be a swift and terrible end. Many will follow their evil teaching that there is nothing wrong with sex sin. And because of them, Christ and His way will be scoffed at" (TLB).

I was not alone in adopting today's morals and standards. Have you attended church lately? Most ministers steer clear of the sin issue. They want attendance. Perhaps they do not deal with sin because they do not have the revelation of God's love and His warning system.

When I experienced major problems in my marriage, the pastor of a major denominational church counseled me. Upon hearing my story, he said, "Donna, when this one goes, you better live with the next one before you marry him."

Jesus said false prophets will "deceive even the elect" (Matt. 24:24). When your own pastor tells you to live in sin, you know the elect is deceived.

At a divorce adjustment workshop at another church in town, I heard a minister using the "f" word naturally. The way he used the word it was descriptive. However, the word still offends me.

Consequently, beginning to stand for what is right will get you ridicule. Beginning to stand for godliness, people will sneer at you. If involved with singles' circles, friends consider your viewpoint Victorian and prudish. You face the possibility of being alone for the rest of your life because you believe as you do. It will even cause you to have doubts whether it's worthwhile.

Rejoice! If you continue and are not faint, if you delight yourself in Him, God says He will bless you. I am expecting blessings. I am expecting my heart's desires. I am not seeking for a husband, but I do expect to God to bless me with one. It will be someone capable of being the spiritual head of my household. If he is, he will be a man of God. If he is a man of God, he will appreciate the stand I am taking which is, after all, biblical.

Looking back on my life, I noticed there are certain things God wanted me to do. Things I might not have done were I married.

This book is a perfect example. Had I married, this book would have been put on the literal back shelf. Also, with God's divine leading, I was responsible for starting an organization. We called the organization Singles Available for Community Service (SACS for short). Volunteering for one-time events for other community service organizations in town, we provide a dignified way for singles to meet one another. The work we do is for the Salvation Army, American Red Cross, United Way, American Heart Association, American Cancer Society, River Parks Authority, Day Center for the Homeless, etc.

I am still amazed how easily this organization came together. God opened doors. Looking back, I know I would not have bothered forming a singles' organization if a man had been in my life.

Is this the reason I'm still single?

God knows what He wants us to accomplish. And He arranges things so we will do what He has sent us to do.

God willingly leads us, but we must willingly follow.

It is impossible to live without sin. However, *we* have hope, in 1 John 1:8-9: "If we say that we have no sin, we deceive ourselves, and the truth is not in us. If we confess our sins, He is faithful and just to forgive us our sins, and to cleanse us from all unrighteousness" (NIV).

And we have hope in 1 John 5:4 (TLB) "For every child of God can obey Him, defeating sin and evil pleasure *by trusting Christ to help him"* (TLB).

I trusted Christ to help me overcome the desire for sex with the man I loved. I trusted Christ to lead the way I should go. He did. And He sent His angels to help.

As mentioned previously, there is some validity to the notion you can have salvation yet not inherit the kingdom of God. The kingdom of God spoken of might very well be the kingdom here on earth. Why take a chance? Remember what it says in I Corinthians 6:9-10: "Know ye not that the unrighteous *shall not inherit* the kingdom of God? Be not deceived: neither *fornicators,* nor idolaters, nor adulterers, nor effeminate, nor abusers of themselves with mankind, nor thieves, nor covetous, nor drunkards, nor revelers, nor extortioners, shall inherit the kingdom of God" (KJV).

This issue of sin could be a fine print on your ticket into the Kingdom in the afterlife. We have all sinned and fallen short, so no one would get into heaven based upon what we do. However, we need to be careful that as Christians we do not continue to walk rebelliously in sin.

In writing this book, I had one concern . . . that if you are not spirit-led, you might believe this book is giving you license to commit the sin of fornication. There are possible eternal promises and problems related to sin: "He that overcometh shall inherit all things; and I will be his God, and he shall be my son. But the fearful and unbelieving, and the abominable, and murderers, and whoremongers [other versions say: 'sexually immoral' (NIV); 'the immoral' (TLB); and 'fornicators' (RSV)], and sorcerers, and idolaters, and all liars, shall have their part in the lake which burneth with fire and brimstone: which is the second death" (Rev. 21:7-8;KJV).

You, as Christian, receive justification by the blood of Jesus, whether or not you are living a totally holy life. God sees you differently. He does not see you as any of the types of people listed above. You have a covering you received from the shed blood of Jesus.

In fact, because of the blood, Satan will pass over you. He'll pass right by, just like he passed the lamb's blood swabbed on Israelite doorposts in Egypt. He sees you as he sees Jesus. You are the same to him because of the blood — UNTIL you open your mouth and say something. What if you open your mouth and say something negative? Will he attack? Probably. You opened the door and gave him a foothold. What if every time you open your mouth you are saying things that line up with the Word of God? Because he sees you as he sees Jesus and with the same authority as Jesus, he'll flee — maybe not immediately. He'll hang around long enough to test you. It could be years. God wants to know you will continue to believe, no matter what the circumstances.

We all know God works in each life in a totally unique way. He cleanses different areas at different times with different people, and He will do it in His time. It is not possible to be completely and totally changed in one day. You are to renew your mind daily and change will come daily. God sees you as sinless because He remembers sins no more. "Then he adds: 'Their sins and lawless acts I will remember no more' " (Heb. 10:17).

Even if you are still living with sin in your life, you are sanctified and made pure. You received this blessing of forgiveness because you decided to believe in the One God sent in the flesh. Is not one of the categories mentioned as having their part in the lake of fire the unbelievers?

If you "overcometh," you shall "inherit ALL things," those

things here on earth as well as in heaven. The phrase "hang in there" comes to mind.

It's as though God places a governor in you that tells you exactly how fast to go. Eventually, you will *want* to please God, because you will realize that *pleasing God pleases you.*

God's will is for you to live a holy life:

> It is God's will that you should be holy; that you should avoid sexual immorality, that each of you should learn to control his own body in a way that is holy and honorable, not in passionate lust like the heathen who do not know God; and that in this matter no one should wrong his brother or take advantage of him. The Lord will punish men for all such sins, as we have already told you and warned you. For God did not call us to be impure, but to live a holy life. Therefore, he who rejects this instruction does not reject man but God, who gives you the Holy Spirit (1 Thess. 4:3-8;NIV).

There is something positive you could do for yourself. You could separate yourself from the elements and the people contributing directly or indirectly to your destruction. If someone "wrongs" you in this way, you should run, not walk, to the nearest exit. If you do not, you are on a dead-end road that leads to unhappiness.

Why? Because of what God says in this Scripture. If anyone wrongs his brother or takes advantage of him in sexual immorality, the Lord will punish him. If God is punishing someone around you, you might be caught in the aftermath. Can your angels work at maximum capacity when surrounded by demons?

This does make me wonder about the roll of the "aggressor" versus "aggressee." In other words, it seems to me that a seduced woman is not wronging her brother, but her brother is wronging her, right?

"It was impossible," Shana told me. Shana's Irish, and her black hair, luminescent azure eyes, and nearly snow white complexion are a rarity and a pleasure to behold. Should she flash a smile with her Julia Robert's lips, any man would be enthralled. "If positions reversed, would he have been able to withstand the same seduction? My goodness, he caressed me, held me, fondled me. . . . And I pulled away. I said no. And I said no. And I said no. Over and over again I said no. But it was so comforting to be held again."

I knew what she meant. This previous sexual experience we have could be a dangerous thing.

"He just kept pursuing. I could not withstand the pressure. I gave in."

Shana walked to the sink in her Broken Arrow apartment to pour us each a mug of black coffee as she continued her story.

"I've got to tell you, Donna, I enjoyed it. For several weeks we continued to date. Once you have opened the barn door, it is impossible to shut again."

Returning to the table, leaning elbows on the yellow formica top, Shana looked thoughtful. She continued. "We dated for a few more weeks. He was calling me sometimes four and five times a day. It was so pleasant. But I had to stop it. I could not take the pressure any longer. . . . The inner voice just kept hammering at me, night and day, hammering at me. I sent him packing. I tried to remain friends and we've succeeded at that about as well as any ex-lovers. He shows up in church once in a while, always with another lady on his arm."

"How does that make you feel?" I asked, curiously.

"Thankful. I was the first person he dated after his divorce. I know sooner or later he would have dumped me. This affair was as close as I have ever come to enjoying sport sex."

"Why do you say that? You didn't care for him?"

"Sure, I cared. But I knew the odds. I protected myself. But even with the intellectual knowledge that it would end, I was still becoming bonded to him. There was still a ripping of my spirit when it ended."

What will happen to this man if he continues this method in his pursuit of pleasure? I wouldn't particularly want to be around him. He will probably be punished in some way. After all, bad company corrupts good character (1 Cor. 15:33).

And it is especially important to steer clear if this person calls himself a Christian who wrongs his sister in this way (1 Cor. 5:11). Why would this be so? God does not want you taken in by their ideas and encouraged to make the wrong choices as Shana did.

Of course, good company promotes good character.

One way to become whole is to avail yourself of people, classes, church, and all avenues available for the transformation of your mind and your lifestyle. There is a nationally known public speaker who makes millions teaching people this one principle. He says if you want to be successful at something, associate with someone who is.

Not all the people you meet in the church are going to be as healthy as you are. That may be the very reason you are there, to help those less fortunate. There are those who know more than you — find a way to get to know them.

Someone recently said sparrows fly in flocks, but eagles fly alone. Eagles, you are needed in the church. An eagle might teach a sparrow to soar.

You may be an angel sent to minister to someone else.

Assured by the Word

Are you hung by your tongue or assured by the Word?

Confess nothing but the Word of God about yourself, no matter what the circumstances in your life. Recognize the situation, then *YOU* (it's your job) put God's Word to work on it.

The only way the devil can tell he is succeeding is when you open your mouth. The devil is a fallen angel. He has no ability to read your mind. He can put thoughts into your mind. You can choose to dwell on those thoughts or not. But he cannot read your mind. It is only when your mouth is open and your lips are moving that he can see his success or failure in your life.

Think of it this way: What if you received everything that came out of your mouth from now on? Would you say some of the things you are saying now?

Speaking God's Word produces faith. Faith comes through hearing. That means you must speak it. Pick Scriptures related to your area of concern. Personalize those Scriptures. Repeat them to yourself several times a day, three times each, like this:

Say to the devil: "It is written."
Say to the Lord: "Your Word says."
Say to yourself: "And I believe."
For example, using Psalm 60:6:

Devil, it is written "God has promised to help us. He has vowed it by His holiness. No wonder I exult!"

Lord, Your Word says, "You, God, have promised to help me. You have vowed it by Your holiness. No wonder I exult!"

And I believe, "You, God, have promised to help me. You have vowed it by Your holiness. No wonder I exult!"

When you work with the Word of God, you are armed and ready for battle.

Choose to use the Word.

Chapter 17

Step #7 — From Pitiful to Powerful to Praise!

Enjoy the joy and flourish in God's fullness.

Trials? Temptations? What perspective is your perspective? Is it the human viewpoint? Or do you understand and comprehend the divine viewpoint? The only thing we need to do to please Him (and thus walk free of worry over trials and temptation) is to have faith.

Remember Paula? When she found herself evicted from her home, we can pretty well guess that circumstances were overwhelming. She didn't know what to do. She made no effort to work it out herself. Her mother-in-law made an offer she couldn't refuse. As she was living in that mansion with maid service and gardeners with no cost whatsoever to her, she was awestruck by the way God worked out her problem for her. The fact that now she completely trusts God's miracle-working power has not been lost on her or any of her friends. Had she not had that miracle, she would not have the trust she now has in her Lord.

When I heard her story and when I compared my life, I realized each step along the way I had a Red Sea experience. Circumstances were out of my control, and all seemed hopeless. Yet I'm still here.

How?

Why?

Could it be? Of course!

BIG MIRACLES BUILD BIG FAITH.

Little miracles, things that do not seem to be life or death situations or critical, are nice, indeed. But the Big Miracles — those where it means the difference between survival or not — when big miracles are manifested in your life, you can see God at work. Small miracles grow small faith. With big miracles, the bigger the miracle, the bigger growth of your faith.

David slew first a lion, then a bear, and finally Goliath. Each slaying was progressively larger, so that by the time Goliath came along, he had faith he could slay him, too. So it is with miracles. Each one is progressively larger until you are sure that your faith in God works.

What is God's purpose in this? Those who are greatly used are greatly tested. It is not possible to separate your circumstances from the Lord, for He has allowed them in your life. Nothing happens to you except what is His will. And you are to praise Him in every situation because it is His will for you (1 Thess. 5:16-18). No matter what happens, good, bad, or indifferent, you are to praise Him and speak of all the good things He has done for you (Ps. 34:1-4). You are to count everything for naught except knowing Him. You cannot become His disciple unless you first sit down and count your blessings — and then renounce them all for Jesus.

And we know that all who seek the Lord shall find Him and shall praise His name. And our hearts shall rejoice with everlasting joy. This is a promise you can stand on and accept as you seek the Lord.

About joy, it meant a great deal to Jesus that you have joy in your life. He mentions it in John 15:7-8: "If ye abide in me, and my Words abide in you, ye shall ask what ye will, and it shall be done unto you. Herein is My Father glorified, that ye bear much fruit; so shall ye be my disciples" (KJV).

To Jesus it is important for you to have answered prayers. The key is abiding in His Word. When you know His Word, then you know whether or not your prayers line up with His Word. You ask only those things that line up with His Word. And we know if we ask anything according to His Word, He hears us and we have the petitions we desire. We need only believe.

Matthew Henry, the eighteenth century writer, agrees with me. He states: "Those that abide in Christ as their heart's delight shall have, through Christ, their heart's desire. If we abide in Christ, and His Word in us [John 15:7-8], we shall not ask anything but what is proper to be done for us. The promises abiding in us lie ready to be turned into prayers; and the prayers so regulated cannot but speed."[17]

This is further confirmed in John 15:11: "I have told you this so that my joy may be in you and that *your joy may be full.*"

And just to be absolutely certain you have in your spirit the knowledge of the joy God wants for you, Jesus repeats it yet again: "Verily, verily, I say unto you, Whatsoever ye shall ask the Father in my name, he will give it you. Hitherto have ye asked nothing in my name: ask, and ye shall receive, *that your joy may be full*" (John 16:23-24;KJV).

Don't pass this over without realizing that His Father will not be glorified if you do not bear fruit. And not just some fruit, but much fruit. It is important to God that your prayers be answered. His Word is at stake. His name is to be glorified. This is why I wanted to know Christ. I wanted to have the same peace of mind, the same happiness, the same joy, the same fruit that I saw in the lives of Christians I knew.

God inhabits your praises.

"Yet you are enthroned as the Holy One; you are the praise of Israel" (Ps. 22:3).

And with the praises of God on your lips you can stand in any circumstance. In every circumstance, God's purpose is that we should praise Him and give Him glory for doing mighty things for us.

So, when you are faced with these circumstances, when that man is there before you, tempting you to succumb, remember when you praise God, turn away, and trust Him, He will have something better for you. And your joy will be full. That's a promise.

You will feel pitiful when you give up that man. But you will become powerful as you learn to praise.

Then simply enjoy your joy and flourish in His fullness.

You Can't Sit Down

In the Old Testament the children of Israel roam the desert for 40 years. During all that time the Lord fed them with manna which settled on the ground like dew in the night. That daily bread was symbolic of our Lord Jesus Christ.

The children of Israel received the bread from heaven, but they had a job to do. They had to go out and get that bread each day, once in the morning and once in the evening. They could only take enough for that day. If they gathered more than they needed, leaving some for the next morning, it would rot. The exception was the Sabbath. God told the children of Israel to gather enough to last through the Sabbath day. That manna did not rot the second day as it did any other day of the week.

What this tells me is God's chosen ones had to put forth an effort each day to receive their daily bread. They had to go out in the morning and in the evening.

God would not feed the Israelites the manna, but He would supply the manna.

God does not force-feed us His Word, but He does supply.

I imagine every time the Israelites went out to gather the manna they thanked God for the provision. At least until they began to take it for granted. Then the manna became polluted, changing colors, when they began to complain rather than praise.

We cannot sit down, either. To get our daily provision, we need make to an effort. We cannot take His provision for granted and expect Him to be pleased. We are to put on our full armor (Eph. 6:10-18) to fight the devil's schemes. And you must do it daily. It's not enough once weekly, but it must be daily. What is your armor?

1) *A belt of truth buckled around your waist.* The Bible tells us if we continue in God's Word, we will know the truth and

the truth sets us free. The truth is, sex is not beneficial to you; long-range you will be hurt if you go against your internal guidance system.

2) *The breastplate of righteousness.* We have been made the righteousness of God by faith in Jesus Christ. Is having sex outside of marriage living in right standing with God?

3) *Feet fitted with the readiness that comes from the gospel of peace.* Do you know the Gospel? Are you ready to preach the Gospel to every creature? When you realize the result of the effort you put into Bible study will be peace of mind, you will put more effort into reading.

4) *Helmet of salvation.* Without salvation, we have nothing. All promises mean nothing to those who do not believe. *Those who believe receive. Those who don't won't.* It really is as simple as that. However there is a chance your name could be blotted out of the book of life (Rev. 3:5). It is a choice you make. Scripture says, "He that overcometh" will not have his name blotted out of the book of life. So, you are in the driver's seat. You simply must decide to overcome with your purpose and decision to do so and His guidance. Like a pilot following the direction of his ground crew, you will make that hangar called heaven. There is no other name under heaven given among men whereby we must be saved (Acts 4:12).

5) *Shield of faith.* Until you begin to act in faith you cannot see faith working for you. God allows circumstances to teach you to rely on Him, to develop your faith. In sexual issues, you must rely on Him to straighten out these issues and leave it in His capable hands.

6) *Sword of the spirit, which is the Word of God.* The Word of God is sharper than any two-edged sword. All you have to do to use the sword is to grab hold and hang on!

Chapter 18

Here Comes the Judge

Once you begin to walk in holiness you might have a tendency to judge others. Your place is not to make any assessments of anyone. In fact, if you judge others, you are going to be judged by the same measuring stick.

"Ouch!" was the response of one man in my Sunday school class after hearing this. A legalist, he enjoys a good game of "Catch Them While You Can." You know the kind. There are groups of them in every church. As a former heathen, this attitude is a real big problem.

The only way to measure your value is by faith. How can you say what is right for your sister?

Like two managers working for the same company, each has an area of responsibility. One manages engineering, the other accounting. For you to tell someone how to run her life is like the manager of engineering trying to direct accounting personnel.

Who you are to manage someone else's employee? To his own manager he stands or falls.

If your friend is managed by the Lord, she will stand. For the Lord is able to make her stand.

Have you ever wondered how Jesus handled sin? I looked up every Scripture I could find. Jesus preached against sins. He taught the masses. He did not directly reprimand a person for sin. He told people, "Go and sin no more." He knew when His people grew convicted in their spirit through His preaching.

Jesus did not point a finger. In fact, the only point where Jesus chastised someone, He placed the blame elsewhere. A lie coming from Peter, Jesus recognized as from Satan. Jesus did not say, "Get thee behind me, Peter, you are lying and that is a sin."

Our job is fishing for men. Have you noticed that fishermen don't aim at a fish and try to shoot it? They put the bait on a hook, toss it in the water, and wait for the fish to bite. If you want people to bite on your bait, you need to make it tantalizing and worthwhile. As one person recently put it, "You have to bait the hook to suit the fish." Judgment, condemnation, and legalism do not bait the hook to suit any fish I know.

If there is obvious sin in the life of a professing Christian, we Christians should handle the situation as the Bible says: "Dear brothers, if a Christian is overcome by some sin, you who are godly should gently and humbly help him back onto the right path, remembering that next time it might be one of you who is in the wrong. Share each other's troubles and problems, and so obey our Lord's command" (Gal. 6:1-2;TLB).

Your position is not to judge your sister, even if you know her to be in sexual sin. Your position is to help. You can help in several ways:

1) You can advise her (Matt. 18:15-17).

2) You can tell her what the Scriptures say about this sin.

3) You can give her a copy of this book.

4) You can avoid her and not invite her to lunch so you will not be persuaded to her way of thinking (1 Cor. 5:9-12). This, too, is for her benefit. Regarding a church member who is liv-

ing in sin the Bible says: "Cast out this man from the fellowship of the church and into Satan's hands, to punish him, in the hope that his soul will be saved when our Lord Jesus Christ returns" (1 Cor. 5:5;TLB). Tough love.

5) You can take her to church to hear a specific preacher or message.

Have you seen Christian bumper stickers saying, "God's not finished with me yet," or "I'm not perfect, just forgiven"? The following Scripture says there will be a time we will be judged:

> I care very little if I am judged by you or by any human court; indeed, I do not even judge myself. My conscience is clear, but that does not mean I am innocent. It is the Lord who judges me. Therefore, judge nothing before the appointed time; wait till the Lord comes. He will bring to light what is hidden in darkness and will expose the motives of men's hearts. At that time each will receive his praise from God (1 Cor. 4:3-5;NIV).

Praise from God is what you can expect to receive when you, as a Christian, are judged at the judgment seat of God. This goes for your sister, too.

An interesting study is judgment day in the Bible. It appears we Christians are acquitted, we praise our God, we receive rewards. I have not found anywhere it says we will receive punishment. We will be given credit for those things we did right, not what we did wrong. After all, Jesus cleansed us as white as snow and our sins are remembered no more. What is there to judge?

In the book *Angels on Assignment*, written by Charles and Frances Hunter as told by Roland Buck, Roland discusses a visit he had to heaven. He says:

> One of the most exciting things to me was the peek that God gave me into Abraham's and

Sarah's records. . . . One thing I could not find was the places where Abraham stumbled. . . .

"God, where is the other book?"

"I have no other book for the believers."

"Where did you write about the failures of Abraham which I have seen recorded in your own words in the Bible?"

"I have no other book. *I do not record failure in heaven!*"[18]

The book refers us to Hebrews 10:17-18, which says: "Then he adds: 'Their sins and lawless acts I will remember no more' " (NIV).

Remember that small voice within you that speaks to you occasionally? In Galatians 5:16 Paul tells why: "I advise you to obey only the Holy Spirit's instructions. He will tell you where to go and what to do, and then you won't always be doing the wrong things your evil nature wants you to. When you are guided by the Holy Spirit you need no longer force yourself to obey Jewish laws" (TLB).

Further, Paul says: "For the sinful nature desires what is contrary to the Spirit, and the Spirit what is contrary to the sinful nature. They are in conflict with each other, so that you do not do what you want. But if you are led by the Spirit, you are not under law" (Gal. 5:17-18;NIV).

No Christian is under the law, not you or your sister. So how can you judge your sister by the law? It is not your place.

One word of caution. We are in the end times. It should be obvious to any Bible student who has studied prophecy. So, it is extremely *selfish* of us not to help our brothers and sisters to see God's way. Our job is to gently guide them *for their own good*. We are to show others love. Jesus is coming back for a spotless bride. And thankfully all children of God are spotless when we are covered by Jesus's atoning blood. He uses us, his vessels, to speak the truth to others. If we do not tell someone else what the Bible says, we fail in our mission.

How do you share this information with another? Do you inform with love and understanding, or do you do it with censure, condemnation, and disapproval? Do you realize how diffi-cult it is to move away from sexual situations? Do you under-stand how the natural mind cannot believe they could ever be free? Do you realize it is not an act of will, but an act of purpose? If you are reading this book, odds are you understand.

Your job is to do what God prompts you to do. A simple thing to remember is, if it causes you confusion, it is not of God, for God is not the author of confusion. If there is any doubt, don't do it.

It is God's job to bring the right people in a person's path, and it might be you. It is God's job to open the eyes of someone's understanding. It is God's job to cause them to become willing. God will do his part. Sometimes the change is immediate. Some-times it takes time. We, as God's vessels, should leave the timing to Him.

You will find some who worry so about other people's sal-vation, they are not willing to consider their own. They worry about the Hindus and the Muslims and the Aborigines. Jesus said, "If I had not come and spoken to them, they would not be guilty of sin [the amplified says they would be blameless]. Now, how-ever, they have no excuse for their sin" (John 15:22;NIV).

So, tell such these worried people to relax. And ask them, "What about you?"

In another Scripture Paul says, "For the truth about God is known to them instinctively; God has put this knowledge in their hearts. Since earliest times men have seen the earth and the sky and all God made, and have known of his existence and great eternal power. So they will have no excuse [when they stand before God at Judgment Day]" (Rom. 1:19-20;TLB).

Jesus is the creator branch of the Trinity according to the first chapter of John. So if we see nature and recognize a God created nature, we recognize Christ. Those who recognize the creator God, and thus recognize Christ, have a covering. Why would anyone let concern over others stop them from receiving all God has for them?.

So, regarding this issue of judging others, you be the judge. Does it make sense to judge anyone else? Does it make sense to judge yourself? What is your verdict?

Chapter 19

It's about That Christian Spouse, God. . . .

Believe me, I know as a woman how hard it is to find a Christian spouse. Is it impossible to find a man capable of being the spiritual head of a household? Sometimes it looks that way.

In my experience, men do not necessarily want to marry. Nor do you find many particularly serious about their Christianity. They realize a requirement might be to "clean up their act." They are having too much fun. All the sex available today for the single man is like Willy Wonka in his chocolate factory. So, women shot themselves in the foot by making it easy for men not to commit.

Discussing this with Harold, who recently married one of my best friends, he agreed. Harold said he and his male friends talked of the problems they faced with women and dating.

They all agreed women expected a move to be made. If a man did not make a move, the woman thought there was something wrong with her or with him. Once the move was made, if they got the woman in bed, they expected emotional blackmail. Expectations. Commitment. These men were not ready.

They would hesitate, Harold said, to even ask a woman out for fear of this outcome. They wondered why you could not have a nice friendship with a woman . . . no sex and no strings.

Rather than dealing with the hassles, these men decided it was better alone.

So, men find themselves in a Catch 22 circumstance as well, damned if they do and damned if they don't. If ground rules were established up front, possibly no one would get hurt.

Dr. Robert Schuller in his book *Be Happy You Are Loved*, said these things about love:

> It's funny about love — when confronted with love of others, most of us hold back. We approach any new relationship hesitantly, suspiciously, and some of us even turn and run away. Why is that? *If love is so beautiful, so profoundly satisfying, so happiness-producing, why doesn't every normal human being instinctively, intuitively, irresistibly race to embrace fellow humans with a holy hug? Why don't we rush headlong into happy relationships?* Could it be that we are afraid? Afraid of rejection? Of failure? Of oppression? — What is the fear? *It is simply lack of faith.*

Dr. Schuller further points out that although love can bring disappointment and pain, it can also bring real possibilities. Real love, he says, encourages the greatness within each of us. "Nothing releases the greatness within people more than love." I am sure you have heard someone say after a divorce they no longer had anyone to work for. Dr. Schuller further states: Give love — and if it's accepted, you have succeeded! If love is rejected, you still have your love to give to someone else who is waiting to accept and *appreciate it.*[19]

Recently, my pastor friend, Gary, shared with me a tape of a talk he gave at a men's meeting. In this speech, Gary listed steps for a Christian marriage. I believe these steps, if followed, would keep 99.9 percent of all the relationships together. He said something very profound. He said these steps were "A platform for you to build a godly relationship, *and not do it alone.*" The point is, why would anyone want to "do it alone?" One can put a thousand to flight and two can put ten thousand to flight. So, it makes logical, even mathematical sense, to work together. And men are logical, so maybe this is something that they could see would be of benefit to them.

Besides, Proverbs 18:22 says, "He who finds a wife finds what is good *and receives favor from the Lord.*"

In sales, I learned to frame conversations in words to show the benefit to the buyer. If a man were to receive favor from the Lord, would that not be benefit enough to find a wife?

Do not get discouraged. If you want to find the spouse God has in store for you, leave it in His hands. Check yourself. Are you born again? Is Jesus Lord of your life? God can find a way.

God specifically dealt with the desire of my heart — to marry happily a Christian husband. He gave me this Scripture: "But be sure in deciding these matters that you are living as God intended, *marrying or not marrying in accordance with God's direction and help* and accepting whatever situation God has put you into. This is my rule for all churches" (1 Cor. 7:17;TLB).

Coming to this conclusion before God gave me this Scripture, I decided to be happy in my situation whatever it might be. Marriage may not be what God has in store for me. He may want me totally involved in His work. I figure if God wants me to have a mate, He's going to have to put him in my path.

One thing the Bible says about wanting to marry — not to seek a spouse. Many have missed this passage, I'm sure. We are told if we are married, not to seek to leave that marriage. And if we do not have a spouse, we are not to seek one (1 Cor. 7:27). Only the Lord can build the right house (Ps. 127:1)

For years and years, I tried to figure out what God had in store for me. I tried to play God. How? I knew that Charles was not capable of becoming the spiritual head of my household. I projected upon Charles a characteristic he did not have. Don't get me wrong. He was most certainly capable of being head of every other area of the household, just not the most important.

We would have been unequally yoked.

So, I've learned, based on "not leaning on my own understanding," to quit trying to figure things out. I have learned to not trust myself.

We already know God's will. If we want a mate, choose to use the Word.

My friend, Lindsay, recently married Harold. Lindsay has been a Christian for ten years. Just before her marriage, Lindsay made decisions similar to mine, that sex outside of marriage was not God's will or His best. She and Harold dated before her decision. Harold, a "baby Christian," had only become a Christian a year earlier.

Lindsay told Harold she could no longer have sex with him. He was furious. So, he simply resolved the issue by asking her to marry him, and marry him soon. Lindsay was not quite ready to marry, but neither did she want to give up on a loving relationship.

Are you afraid to tell someone you love you have come to this conclusion? The outcome may be what you have been praying for all along.

On the following pages is information that I pray you will find useful. First is a questionnaire about a future mate with an example completed form. Next are scriptural confessions you can make for a mate. Also enclosed is the information for the man searching for a wife. You need to know what Scripture says is your partnership position. The poem tells us we need to rely on God, especially for a Christian mate.

Relationship Survey
(with sample answers)

1) What traits do I look for in the opposite sex?

    A) Someone capable of being spiritual head of my household.

    B) Someone with self-confidence.

    C) Someone I can respect and look up to.

    D) Someone I can trust.

    E) Someone who is decisive.

    F) Someone who allows me to be me, with whom I

can be comfortable.

G) Someone with intelligence and common sense.

H) Someone with a sense of humor.

I) Someone who can share his feelings with me and force me to do the same.

J) Someone with an uncritical nature and who is tolerant.

K) Someone with a neat, attractive appearance.

L) Someone happy with themselves and their lot in life.

M) Someone at least as successful as I am.

N) Someone who enjoys *some* of the same things I enjoy.

O) Someone who is not an alcohol or drug user; non-smoker preferable.

2) In a PERFECT relationship, what do I want my partner to do for me?

A) Someone whose ministry gifts merge with mine and enjoys church as I do.

B) Willing to go places with me from time-to-time just because I want to go, and do it without complaining.

C) Someone who will not smother me, but who will let me know daily that he is thinking about me with a phone call.

D) Someone who will listen to me and support me in my job, who will make positive suggestions, but not personally interfere in my career — OR — perhaps someone who is in a ministry or profession with which I can be of benefit.

E) Someone who will share with me his concerns and his successes and allow me to offer positive suggestions, but not personally interfere.

F) Someone who will include themselves in my daughter's life, but who will accept her as she is and allow me to continue to discipline and train her as I see fit with suggestions accepted.

G) Someone who is my best friend, with whom I

can share my inner-most feelings and thoughts.

H) Someone who has that indefinable ability to make me feel cherished and special.

I) Someone who makes me feel protected, who will be willing to make the major decisions in the family, with my help, but he will have the final say over family decisions, but will not try to tell me exactly what to do.

3) What would I be willing to do for my partner in return?

A) Would be loyal.

B) Would be supportive.

C) Would be willing to go wherever he wants, to do whatever he wants, whenever he wants MOST OF THE TIME, especially if I am not working outside the home.

D) Will move where he wants to move.

E) Will be supportive of his career and the demands of his career.

F) Will involve myself with his family, if he wants me to do so, and allow them to have access to our home as they would their own home with their own mother.

G) Will accept him as he is and not try to change him.

H) Will be open and honest with regard to my feelings.

I) Will do all I can to show that I respect him, as long as I do respect him. But as a Christian, I must see that I respect my husband before I marry him.

4) What are turn-ons?

A) Someone who loves the Lord.

B) Self-Confidence.

C) Sense of humor.

D) Eye contact.

E) Being held close, dancing cheek-to-cheek.

F) Holding hands for no reason.

G) A single rose.

H) Someone who challenges me (iron sharpens iron).

I) Someone who opens my doors for me and generally treats me like a lady.

J) Being romanced.

5) What are turn-offs?

A) Someone who is not saved.

B) Drunkenness/alcoholism/drug abuse.

C) Crude language.

D) Lewd insinuations, talking of going to bed or having sex.

E) Someone who hints that he might be interested, but who never really does anything about it.

6) What is a pet peeve on a first date?

A) Sexual insinuations and discussions.

B) Someone who says he will call, and he does not intend to do so.

7) What traits do I possess that I believe are pleasing to the opposite sex?

A) Love of the Lord.

B) Honesty.

C) Discretion.

D) Happy spirit.

E) Not jealous.

F) Not a clinging vine.

G) Attractive in a wholesome way.

H) Common sense.

I) Willing to try new things and take risks.

J) Ability to make the man I love feel good about himself.

8) What traits do I feel I need to improve upon before I make a good partner in a relationship?

A) Must learn to become less independent. Want to turn over the reigns, but wouldn't really know how.

B) Better organize my time and resources and set priorities.

The answers to the following questions must obviously be your own.

9) What have I learned from past relationships and/or marriages that has influenced by present relationship decisions?

10) Do I only date people who I know are suitable for long-term relationships and/or marriage? Why or why not?

11) Do I really want a long-term relationship and/or marriage? Why?

Trusting for a Mate

Single Woman Trusting for a Mate

Below is a prayer and specific Scriptures for the single woman trusting God for a mate. These Scriptures are personalized. When you speak these out loud you will be speaking the Word of God. It will get the Word into your spirit, renewing your mind to God's will for you. It will build your faith. Faith comes by hearing, and hearing by the Word of God.

Father, in the name of Your Son, Jesus Christ, I believe You have provided Your very best for me, and the man that You have planned to be united with me in holy matrimony has awakened to righteousness. As You have rejoiced over Jerusalem, Father, I pray so shall this bridegroom rejoice over me. Thank You, Father, that my husband will love me as Christ loves the Church. He will nourish, carefully protect, and cherish me. I believe that doubts, wavering, and insincerity are not a part of my husband, and he speaks forth Your oracles, God, acknowledging Your full counsel with all wisdom and knowledge. My husband does not speak or act contrary to Your Word. He walks totally in love, esteeming and preferring others higher than himself. Father, I believe that everything not of You shall be removed from my life. And I thank You for the perfecting of Your Word in my life that I may be thoroughly furnished unto all good works. Father, I praise You for the performance of Your Word in my behalf and on behalf of every other single woman I know. (Scripture references are Isaiah 62:5; Ephesians 5:25; James 3:17; Proverbs 8:8.)

Genesis 2:18 — My husband will know that it isn't good for him to be alone, and that I am to be his helpmate.

Genesis 2:23-24 — And I am bone of my husband's bones and flesh of his flesh; I shall be called "woman," for I was taken out of man. For this reason my husband will leave his father and mother and will be united with me, his wife, and we will become one flesh.

Psalm 127:1 — Lord, I believe that unless You build the house, its builders labor in vain.

Proverbs 2:11-16 — Discretion watches over my husband and keeps him away from alien women and from the outsiders with their flattering words.

Proverbs 5:15 — My husband and I will drink waters out of our own cistern of pure marriage relationship, and fresh running water out of our own well.

Proverbs 5:19 — My husband will be absolutely transported with delight in my love and my bosom will satisfy him at all times.

Proverbs 12:4 — I will be a wife of noble character and my husband's crown.

Proverbs 18:22 — My husband will realize that if he finds me as his wife that he finds a good thing and finds favor with the Lord.

Ecclesiastes 9:9 — My husband will live happily with me, the woman he loves, through the fleeting days of life, for the wife (me) You, God, give my husband is his best reward down here for all his earthly toil.

Isaiah 34:16 — I will not want (lack) for my mate in fulfillment, for Your mouth, Lord, has commanded and Your Spirit gathers us together.

Isaiah 54:5 — For You, Lord, the Creator, will be my husband. The Lord of Hosts is Your name. You are my Redeemer, the Holy One of Israel, the God of all the earth.

Romans 15:5-7 — My husband and I will live in mutual

harmony and full sympathy with one another, that we will always with one voice and one heart praise and glorify You, Lord, Father of our Lord Jesus Christ.

1 Corinthians 7:17 — Lord, I want to live as you intended, marrying or not marrying in accordance with Your direction and help and accepting whatever situation You have put me into.

1 Corinthians 11:7-9 — God, Your glory is man in Your image and man's glory is the woman. For man did not come from woman but woman from man; neither was man created for woman but woman for man.

1 Corinthians 11:11 — I remember that in Your plan, God, men and women need each other.

1 Corinthians 13:4-7 — Love is very patient and kind, never jealous or envious, never boastful or proud, never haughty or selfish or rude. Love does not demand its own way. It is not irritable or touchy. It does not hold grudges and will hardly even notice when others do it wrong. It is never glad about injustice, but rejoices whenever truth wins out. If I love someone I will be loyal to him no matter what the cost. I will always believe in him, always expect the best of him, and always stand my ground defending him.

2 Corinthians 6:14 — I will not be unequally yoked with an unbeliever; for what fellowship hath righteousness with unrighteousness? What communion has light with darkness?

Ephesians 5:25 — My husband will love me even as Christ also loved the Church.

Ephesians 5:31 — My husband and I will become one flesh.

Ephesians 5:33 — My husband will love me as he loves his own body and I will respect him as my husband.

Philippians 1:27 — My husband and I will stand firm and united in spirit striving side by side, contending with one mind and one purpose for the gospel's sake.

Colossians 3:18 — I will submit myself to my husband as it is fit in the Lord.

1 Timothy 5:8 — My husband will provide for his own house.

2 Timothy 2:22 — I will have faith and love, and enjoy the companionship of those who love You, Lord, and have pure hearts.

1 Peter 3:1-2 — As a wife, I will fit into my husband's plans; for then if he refuses to listen when I talk to him about You, Lord, he will be won by my respectful, pure behavior. My godly life will speak to him better than any words.

1 Peter 3:7 — My husband will honor me as unto the weaker vessel as heirs together of the grace of life, so that his prayers will not be hindered.

Single Man Trusting for a Mate

Below are Scriptures for the man trusting God for a mate. These, too, are personalized. A woman repeating these will become increasingly more aware of her position and responsibility in a Christian marriage. A man repeating these Scriptures will discover those traits he is to look for in a wife.

> Father, in the name Your Son, Jesus Christ, I believe that You have provided me with Your very best, a suitable helpmate. According to Your Word, I believe You have provided a helpmate who will adapt herself to me, respect, honor, prefer, and esteem me. I believe You are providing someone who will stand firmly by my side, united in spirit and purpose, having the same love and being in full accord and of one harmonious mind and intention. Father, in Your Word You say that a wise, understanding, and prudent wife is from You, and he who finds a true wife finds a good thing and obtains favor with You. Father, I know that I have found favor in Your sight, and I praise You and thank You for Your Word, knowing that You watch over it to perform it. (Scripture is from Ephesians 5:22-23; Proverbs 18:22; Proverbs 19:14; Philippians 2:2.)

Genesis 2:18 — My wife will know that it isn't good for her to be alone, and that she is to be my helpmate.

Genesis 2:23-24 — And my wife is bone of my bone and flesh of my flesh; she shall be called "woman," for she was taken out of man. For this reason, I will leave my father and mother and will be united with my wife, and we will become one flesh.

Psalm 127:1 — Lord, I believe that unless You build the house, its builders labor in vain.

Psalm 128:1-3 — Blessings are on me because I reverence and trust You, Lord. I obey You. My reward shall be prosperity and happiness. My wife shall be contented in my home.

Proverbs 5:15 — My wife and I will drink waters out of our own cistern of pure marriage relationship, and fresh running water out of our own well.

Proverbs 12:4 — My wife will be of noble character and my crown.

Ecclesiastes 9:9 — I will live happily with my wife, the woman I love, through the fleeting days of life, for the wife You, God, give me is my best reward down here for all my earthly toil.

Romans 15:5-7 — My wife and I will live in mutual harmony and full sympathy with one another, that we will always with one voice and one heart praise and glorify You, Lord, Father of our Lord Jesus Christ.

1 Corinthians 7:17 — Lord, I want to live as You intended, marrying or not marrying in accordance with Your direction and help and accepting whatever situation You have put me into.

1 Corinthians 11:7-9 — God, Your glory is man in Your image and man's glory is the woman. For man did not come from woman but woman from man; neither was man created for woman but woman for man.

1 Corinthians 11:11 — I remember that in Your plan, God, men and women need each other.

1 Corinthians 13:4-7 — Love is very patient and kind, never jealous or envious, never boastful or proud, never haughty or selfish or rude. Love does not demand its own way. It is not irritable or touchy. It does not hold grudges and will hardly even notice when others do it wrong. It is never glad about injustice, but rejoices whenever truth wins out. If I love someone I will be loyal to her no matter what the cost. I will always believe in her, always expect the best of her, and always stand my ground defending her.

2 Corinthians 6:14 — I will not be unequally yoked to-

gether with an unbeliever; for what fellowship hath righteousness with unrighteousness? What communion has light with darkness?

Ephesians 5:25 — I will love my wife even as Christ also loved the Church.

Ephesians 5:31 — My wife and I will become one flesh.

Ephesians 5:33 — I will love my wife as I love my own body and she will respect me as her husband.

Philippians 1:27 — My wife and I will stand firm and united in spirit striving side by side, contending with one mind and one purpose for the gospel's sake.

1 Timothy 5:8 — I will provide for my own house.

2 Timothy 2:22 — I will have faith and love, and enjoy the companionship of those who love You, Lord, and have pure hearts.

1 Peter 3:7 — I will honor my wife as unto the weaker vessel as heirs together of the grace of life, so that my prayers will not be hindered.

The Poem

Author Unknown

Everyone longs to give themselves completely to someone,
To have a deep soul relationship with another,
To be loved thoroughly and exclusively.
But, GOD, to a Christian, says, "No, not until you are satisfied, fulfilled, and content with being loved by ME alone,
with giving yourself totally and unreservedly to ME,
with having an intensely personal and unique relationship with ME alone,
discovering that only in ME is your satisfaction to be found,
only then will you be capable of the perfect human relationship that I have planned for you.
You will never be united with another until you are united with ME,

exclusive of anyone or anything else, exclusive of any other desires or longings.

I want you to stop planning, stop wishing, and allow ME to give you the most thrilling plan existing, one that you can't imagine.

I want you to have the best.

Please allow ME to bring it to you.

You just keep watching ME expecting the greatest things.

Keep experiencing the satisfaction I am.

Keep listening and learning the things I tell you.

You just wait.

That's all.

Don't be anxious.

Don't worry.

Don't look around at the things others have gotten or that I have given them.

Don't look at the things you think you want.

You just keep looking up to ME or you'll miss what I want to show you.

And then, when you're ready,

I'll surprise you with a love far more wonderful than any you would dream of.

You see, until you are ready and until the one I have for you is ready (I am working even at this moment to have both of you ready at the same time), until you are both satisfied, you won't be able to experience the love that exemplifies your relationship with ME, and this is the perfect love.

And dear one, I want you to have this most wonderful love.

I want you to see in the flesh a picture of your relationship with ME and to enjoy materially and concretely the everlasting union of beauty, perfection, and love that I offer you with MYSELF.

Know that I love you utterly.

I am God

Believe it and be satisfied.

Chapter 20

Are You a Learned Fool?

A learned fool is someone who learns something, and simply remembers it. A fool may claim an open mind. It may be so open it is empty and information flows right through with little revelation or application.

I know this is hard. Sometimes I, too, want to scream, "This is too hard. I don't want to do it anymore." I may even fail to take my own advice someday, but I am trusting God to lead me. If I do fall short of the mark, I have His guarantee to forgive me.

When I first started writing this book, the Lord gave me a vision. In that vision, was a burning bed. It was totally engulfed in flames. Yet people were climbing into that bed, happily joining each other on that bed of flames. I saw myself climbing in. My first response was, "No, not me. God willing, that won't be me."

We have all sinned and come short. A preacher recently said, "The Lord expects me to know and teach His Word. He knows I cannot live it all the time. Thank God I don't have to live up to it because I don't know how."

Do any of us really know how?

Thank God, He understands I am only human. Thank God, I realize He will not kick me out of heaven. Thank God, I know He simply wants me to be happy.

* * *

If you have a revelation or application about this subject, I would like to hear your story. Please write to me:

Donna M. Cowan
2808 South 111th East Avenue
Tulsa, OK 74129-7673

NOTES

[1] Harry Odum, *The Vital Singles Ministry* (Nashville, TN: Abingdon Press, 1992).

[2] Bruce A. Chadwick and Tim B. Heaton, editors, *Statistical Handbook on the American Family* (Phoenix, AZ: Oryx Press, 1992), p. 61, 173.

[3] "Free to Be Family," Family Research Council, Washington, DC, p. 37.

[4] Chadwick and Heaton, *Statistical Handbook on the American Family*, p. 196.

[5] Viktor Frankle, *Man's Search for Meaning* (New York, NY: Simon & Schuster, 1984), p. 66.

[6] Robert Coles and Geoffrey Stokes, *Sex and the American Teenager* (New York, NY: Harper & Row, 1985), p. 72, 82, 101.

[7] Tim Stafford, *Sexual Chaos* (Downers Grove, IL: InterVarsity Press, 1989, 1993), p. 17-18.

[8] Coles and Stokes, *Sex and the American Teenager*, p. 82.

[9] Stafford, *Sexual Chaos*, p. 113-114.

[10] Dayspring Cards, Outreach Publications, Siloam Springs, AR.

[11] Stafford, *Sexual Chaos*, p. 42.

[12] Nancy Honeytree, "Tell Me What Love Is, Jesus," song lyrics used with permission. Ft. Wayne, IN, Honeytree/Windsong Ministries, Inc.

[13] "How to Stand Against Evil," *Word News and Victory Report,* Fall 1992, Victory Christian Center, Tulsa, OK.

[14] Dave Barry, "Check How Guys Think," Knight-Ridder Service, New York, NY.

[15] Norvel Hayes, *Putting Your Angels to Work* (Tulsa, OK: Harrison House Publishers, 1989), p. 193-197.

[16] Hayes, *Putting Your Angels to Work.*

[17] Matthew Henry, edited by Dr. Leslie F. Church, *Matthew Henry's Commentary in One Volume* (Grand Rapids, MI: Zondervan Publishing House, 1961), p. 699, 1594, 1595, 1793.

[18] Henry, *Matthew Henry's Commentary in One Volume.*

[19] Charles and Frances Hunter, *Angels on Assignment* (Kingwood, TX: Hunter Books, 1979), p. 257-258.

[20] Dr. Robert Schuller, *Be Happy You Are Loved* (Nashville, TN: Thomas Nelson, Inc., 1986), p. 263-264.